The Practical Book of

KNIVES

The Practical

Book of KNIVES

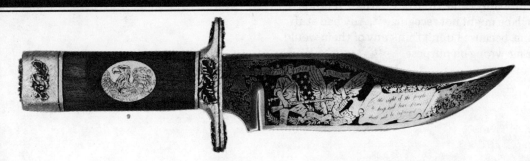

Ken Warner

Stoeger Publishing Company

Acknowledgments

Anyone who has worked with any single subject seriously for fifteen years or so, and written about it, owes a lot of what he knows to a lot of people. That's how it is with me.

I think W. D. Randall, Jr., W. F. Moran, Jr., some fellows named Gerber, Al Buck, Rudy Ruana, Lee Olsen, Jr., Harvey Platts, and R. N. Farquharson hit early licks. R. W. Loveless wrote a lot of useful letters back a ways. With A. G. Russell, it was phone calls.

It wasn't only knifemakers, though. Hunting partners, guides, and a lot of good ol' boys threw grist into my mill. Harry Archer is one of those.

Most of the good stuff—if you find any—in here probably came from one of these fellows, though he might not recognize it. Any bad stuff is mine, because I don't think any of them would steer me wrong on purpose.

Published by Stoeger Publishing Company
55 Ruta Court
South Hackensack, New Jersey 07606

This Stoeger Sportsman's Library edition is published by arrangement with Winchester Press.
Fourth printing, August 1981

Distributed to the book trade and to the sporting goods trade by Stoeger Industries, 55 Ruta Court, South Hackensack, New Jersey 07606

In Canada, distributed to the book trade and to the sporting goods trade by Stoeger Canada, Ltd., 165 Idema Road, Markham, Ontario L3R 1A9

Printed in the United States of America

ISBN 0-88317-025-6

Library of Congress Catalog Card No.: 76-50410

Contents

Introduction

Once I counted something over twenty visible scars on the thumb and forefinger of my left hand. Those scars, most of them faded now, were evidence I had begun learning about knives. I still am. This work is an attempt to shortcut that experience for you in a practical sense, and I hope it works. There won't be any miracle: I cut myself again day before yesterday. You could save some money and time, though.

All at once, it seems, American interest in knives has caught hold. Factory belt knives and pocketknives at $30 and $40 sell like hotcakes, and any fellow who says his handmade knives are worth $100 sells at least some.

Sometimes a $30 knife is a rip-off and sometimes it's a great buy. You have to distinguish between a knife as artifact and the knife as tool, companion, or weapon, and I hope I do here.

There is a very basic fact, germane to all these considerations: $3 or $4 will still buy a knife fully equal to the knives nineteenth-century mountain men carried to live in wild country and fight Indians.

Ken Warner
Falls Church, Va.
February 1976

The Stuff That Knives Are Made Of

1 The blade is the knife and steel is the blade. Apart from nonsteels — such as Stellite — every useful knife blade is, at one time or another, heated red-hot, quenched to brittleness, and then heated again to acquire toughness. The why of this is interesting and the process simple, all of which explains why mass-produced knives are mostly pretty fair cutlery.

For effective use as a knife, a slip of steel — whatever its shape — must be hard enough to take a cutting edge and tough enough to retain that edge for some time in use. A cutting edge is formed when two steel surfaces meet at an angle. The angle they include may be from 10° to 40°. The former will be sharper than the latter, but not nearly so durable in use. How such an edge is obtained will be discussed later. What is important is that it be obtained, and that it last while doing work.

There is hardly any way to appreciate how important the advent of steel was to knife users. It was to other blade materials — bronze, iron, flint — as the machine gun was to the flintlock musket. Before there was steel, of course, the business of the knife went on, but the materials smeared on the grindstone, flaked away under cutting pressure, shattered under a heavy blow, or just bent.

Steel is iron with some additional elements. It has carbon, but sulphur must be limited, for instance. Carbon enables steel to harden; sulphur tends to keep it soft. For centuries, the basic knife steel has had about 1 percent carbon; it may have other alloying elements, too, but the carbon is essential for the molecular changes it makes in the steel when heated and for how that affects the grain structure of the steel.

There have been and continue to be somewhat magical ways to achieve durable sharp edges in steel. Damascus steel, for instance, exemplifies the old magic. It was—and is—a way of intimately combining tough wrought iron with very hard and brittle steel so that the resulting structure provides the best of them both. The Damascus barrels in an old shotgun, incidentally, share only the pattern of what we should call *cutlery* Damascus.

The modern magic involves alloys—tungsten, molybdenum, chromium, and plenty of others—that are, in fact, purposeful additions to the basic high-carbon steel to gain specific advantages. Mostly, these advantages are auxiliary to the basic high-carbon steel's potential.

For example, steel can be alloyed to be abrasion resistant, rust resistant, ductile, variable in weight, softer before heat treatment or harder after heat treatment. This is by no means a complete list, nor can you get all these qualities at the same time. Some alloys are utilized to make fabrication easier and cheaper; some improve the appearance of the finished product; some improve the physical characteristics of the finished product.

There is no such thing as a metallurgical free lunch, so every choice of an alloy of steel is a com-

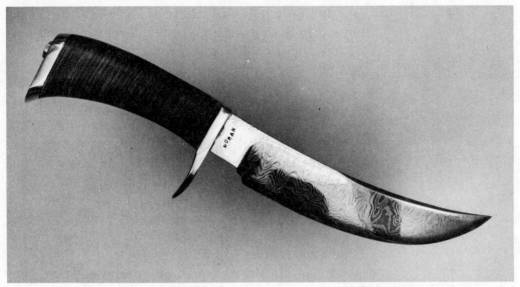

A magic combination of steel and skill results in a Damascus blade like this one by W. F. Moran, Jr., who would be the first to explain that magic is nice, but not needed by today's knife user.

promise. You give something and you get something. All steel technology is available to all users in the United States, and each picks his own compromise. Conversely, you have to get well off base before an alloy of high-carbon steel is wholly unsuitable for cutlery purposes.

Trying to say what steel is best and what to look for in knives is futile. There is only one dividing line in cutlery steel that is important and that is whether your chosen knife has a stainless-steel blade or whether it has not.

Stainless steel isn't stainless, but it damned near is. Personally, I don't care much either way. Some of my best knives are made of stainless steel and it is a definite advantage in maintenance and storage. However, if a knife I like is not stainless steel, I just wipe it off better and go right on using it. Certainly, I have never retired a blade just because it rusts.

Stainless steel does seem more variable than most cutlery steels. Good stuff is great; less than good is lousy. You rarely find cheap good stainless in any class of knife. Maintenance apart, stainless offers one undeniable advantage. If you sharpen such a blade and don't use it, it will still be sharp when you do get around to it. Regular high-carbon steel can suffer oxidation microscopically and lose its edge just sitting around.

Apart from steel, the rest of a knife is handle and guard. Usually the guard and pommel are metal; the gripping surface is something more comfortable to the hand. Brass, nickel-silver, aluminum, pewter, copper, iron, steel, and precious metals are all used for the guard and pommel. Iron is very cheap; copper and pewter are mostly used when other materials are not available. Aluminum solves weight problems when less weight is desired; brass and nickel-silver are handy when more weight is required.

When all else is equal, aluminum gets my vote because it saves weight. My next choice, for romantic reasons, is brass. Brass, wood, and steel look good together to my eye. Still there is no denying that nickel-silver and stainless steel are the two high-class materials these days.

Precious metals? Well, I have some knives with lots of silver on them. It's OK, I suppose, and the glamour of $4-an-ounce silver and $150-an-ounce gold is undeniable. In practical terms, precious metals just mean a whole lot of weight and not quite the strength—if strength is needed—of brass.

Plating, for one effect or the other, of various parts of a knife doesn't make a whole lot of sense to me. When it is very high-quality plating, such as Gerber used back when they made shiny belt knives, it works. But in the main, most plating goes over metal that would work just as well unplated. It is a way to achieve a different color for metal knife parts.

Material for handles comes from everywhere. The horns and bones and teeth of one animal or another have been favorites as long as there have been knives. Wood is another standby. And minerals such as jade get used, too.

Stag horn—made of the antlers of almost every

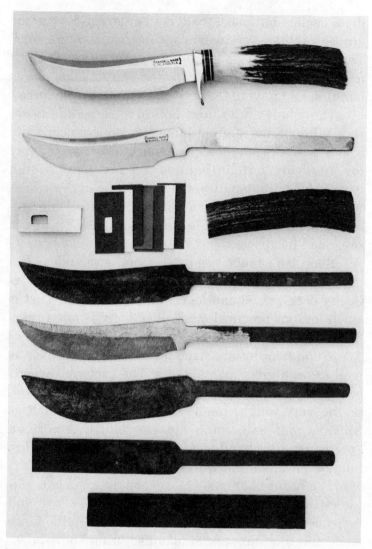

With only minor differences, any knife made goes through the progression shown here that results in a Randall #4 Big Game model.

kind of deer — has been nearly a standard handle material for several centuries. It is hardly ever a bad choice, whether used in flat scales or in the round. It's sturdy and handsome and feels good in the hand. The differences between one kind of stag and another are minor, but present. India stag has a dark reddish color and is relatively smooth; wapiti (elk) horn is gray-brown and rough; the antler material used on the Continent is similar. The antlers of whitetail and mule deer tend to have spongy cores. These don't render them useless but make them neither so solid as others nor so sightly, for instance, on an uncapped butt. That's why you see a lot of the smaller parts—points, for example — of American deer antlers in use as handles. Out toward the ends, the core is not so large.

The whole antler does not serve as handle material, although the straight India stag antlers nearly do. Much of the deer's headpiece curves the wrong way for anything but lefthanded knives. Crown stag means, for knife handles, the butt of the antler where it flares. In order to utilize more of the available antler, some makers assemble handles using short pieces separated by spacers.

Bone isn't much used any more, although it is a practical and handsome material. And ivory has practically been priced and legislated out of sight. That is small loss for practical men, since ivory is not a practical handle material.

Wood handles are standard on working knives as well as on a great many others. The preferred woods are dense and oily tropical species such as rosewood, or the very tough, plain American species such as hickory and ash. Such classier North American species as walnut and maple are nice in knife handles, but are not much in evidence.

The horns of animals other than deer, such as various wild or domestic cattle and sheep, may be found on some imported knives. The material is quite handsome, but requires special manufacturing know-how.

Leather has had a considerable use in the United States. Suitable circles or ovals are cut out of the hide, pierced, and stacked on the tang, then glued together under considerable pressure. When this assembly is dry, it can be shaped by machine. If good dense hides are used, if the glue and pressure are plentiful, and if the assembly is not allowed to get too dry—or to soak and dry out repeatedly—a leather handle can be very comfortable for decades. Eventually, however, it will slacken up. A poor one may do so in a season.

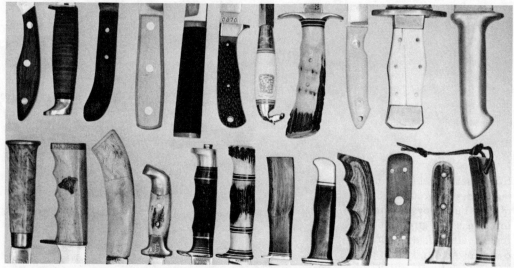

Mineral handles, such as jade or petrified wood, and the similarly textured mother-of-pearl, which is a mineral produced by a mollusc, suffer, as practical handle material, from heavy weight and relative fragility. They can be very, very handsome, however, when properly used.

All of the above are natural products. Naturally enough, knife makers have sought substitutes for them for over a century. The substitutes fall into two easy classifications: imitations of the natural materials and others.

Most faked of the handle materials are stag, horn, pearl, and ivory. Bone was once worked and dyed to look like stag, but most imitation materials are one or another kind of plastic, made in a factory. The truth is that in a rational world most of the imitations would be considered the better materials.

Commercial knife makers in the U.S. may make one or two of their extra-special knives with genuine stag, but that's all. Case does, I know. But it has gotten to the point where there are different grades of imitation stag. In fact, the most common stag imitation is actually an imitation of dyed bone worked to resemble stag!

There are doubtless other common materials used for knife grips not shown here, but not many. Top row, left to right: Wood scales, leather rings, half-tang rosewood, hickory or ash, nylon, Delrin bone, white plastic, India stag with finger grooves, ivory Micarta, ivory (notice cracks), and cast aluminum. Bottom row: Birch root, oosic, bone, cast aluminum with stag, cast plastic, stag, rosewood, plastic resin, impregnated wood, rosewood scales, stag and horn combination, India stag. At least sixteen of these are available on commercial knives.

13

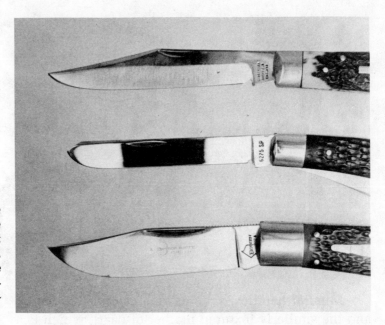

However made, all but a few blades are ground one of these three ways. At the top is a saber grind, not highly polished; at center, a hollow-ground blade with a high finish; at bottom, a flat-ground medium-finish blade.

Horn, pearl, and ivory imitations get more and more successful as their use gets more and more limited. That is to say, they look and feel more and more like the real thing, but fewer people choose them. Actually, a pearl-handled jackknife is easier seen when mislaid than is almost any other.

So soon as there were man-made materials of suitable character, knife makers began to use them for handles. Gutta-percha, hard rubber, and celluloid were early runners. Now, it's nylon, Delrin, one and another form of rubber and rubber substitute, polycarbonate resins, and a host of materials we see in handles and trim and surfaces of all kinds of products and appliances. The classiest plastic handle material today is Micarta, which could be described as thick kitchen-counter covering. It is really tough and stable and relatively "warm" and it works fine. It is dense and so it is heavy, no matter which of its permutations is used.

Micarta comes in solid color, homogeneous in all directions. I've seen black, green, and red, but there are doubtless others. It is also gotten up as an impregnation of various fiber products, chiefly wood and

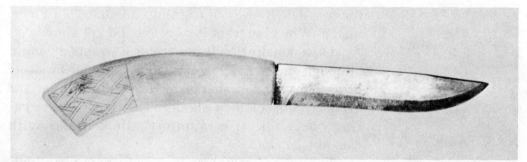

linen. And these are also produced in colors. The wood comes in various wood tones, to and including gray. The linen comes in other colors—black, maroon, and something called, strangely enough, natural. My favorite is natural, which is a creamy yellow to start with and ages sort of orangey, because it has a *real* look to it. Natural linen Micarta looks like something Mother Nature would have provided if she'd thought of it. Maroon and black are quite handsome, too, but don't look as real.

Steel endures. Within limits, it can rust and be rescued, as has been this Norwegian blade. Once the fire gives a piece of steel its character, only fire affects that character again, which is, if we would give it proper weight, magic enough.

There is a laminate, visual texture, looking like the lines on a topographic map, to the linen and wood Micartas — they're all smooth to touch — that helps their looks. When shaped for knife handles, this series of lines can be appealing without being garish.

The materials discussed thus far cover the bulk of the knives made in the world today. In addition, however, there are some pretty wild ideas that you sometimes run across. For example, there is the deer-foot knife, for which the hoof, hide, and a sufficiency of bone of a real deer—usually a roebuck because they're small — is dried out and mounted on a narrow tang knife, the hoof being the pommel. Our own northern Indians went this one better, I think. For a style of broad knife called the beavertail dag, they favored the jawbone—teeth and all—of a bear. (It is possible they cheated with an occasional wolf.)

The burls of tree roots are popular as knife handles in Scandinavia, and many people prefer metal. There is one model of British-made pocketknife with brass scales. By way of warning, it is the Cold Finger model. Why they want it so heavy, I don't know.

Occasionally you'll run across a wrapped handle, although the practice is normally confined to sword grips. I have seen sharkskin, leather, rawhide, and even brocade cloth. I shouldn't be too surprised to find some fellow wrapping knife handles with camouflage cloth.

For me personally, so long as there is plain high-carbon steel, brass, and wood, knives will look and perform just fine. Some nylon and stainless steel for special uses would be nice. And, for variety, an occasional piece of deer antler is sufficient.

Knife Talk

2 Every book on knives must have a chapter on knife terminology and this will be no exception for this is it. However, more pictures and fewer words will be our rule.

There are a great many words that apply to knives; and there are different kinds of knives, each kind having some of its own words. So that it won't remain that simple, there are also synonyms for many of the parts of most of the knives.

The need to have special names for knife parts is plain. It is much easier to say "clip" than "slanting forward edge of the back of the blade, meeting the point," or "scales" rather than "the applied flat pieces that form the two sides of the handle." All of the appropriate names for parts of a knife used in this book are illustrated here.

It is also easier to illustrate types of construction detail, since there are many ways to put a knife together, than to explain fully such detail in words. Those construction details not apparent in the vocabulary illustrations are shown separately.

BELT KNIVES

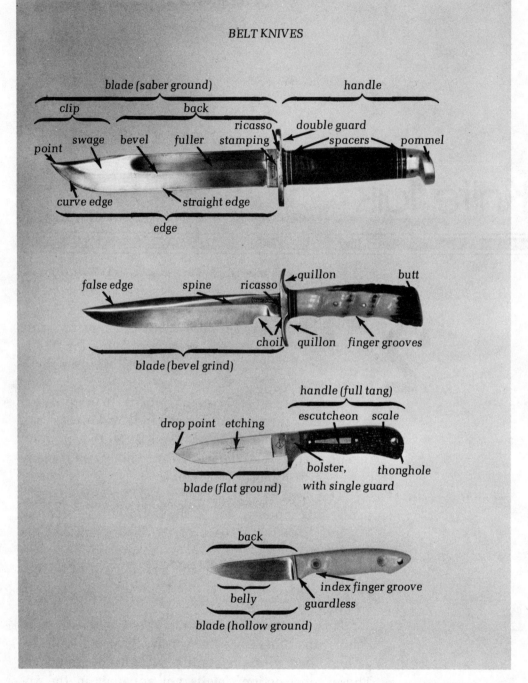

Chart I - Belt Knives

There are uncommon knife features —sawbacks and the like —not shown here, but with these terms clearly in mind, discussion of any belt knife can be clarified.

REGULAR CLIP MASTER BLADE

CUT SWEDGE
NAIL MARK
BACK
POINT
CLIP
BACK SQUARE
SHOULDER
TANG END
EDGE
CHOIL
KICK
TANG FRONT
BLADE TANG

BLADE AND SPRING ACTION

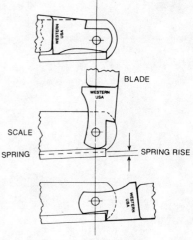

BLADE

SCALE

SPRING

SPRING RISE

3 BLADE STOCKMAN'S POCKET KNIFE

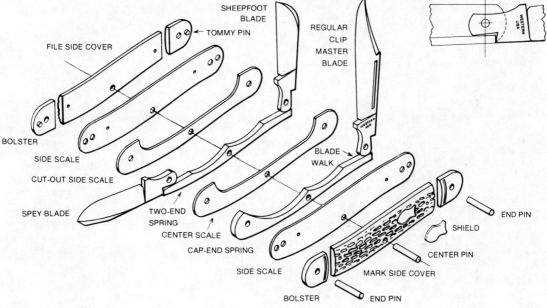

SHEEPFOOT BLADE

TOMMY PIN

FILE SIDE COVER

REGULAR CLIP MASTER BLADE

BOLSTER

SIDE SCALE

CUT-OUT SIDE SCALE

BLADE WALK

SPEY BLADE

TWO-END SPRING

CENTER SCALE

CAP-END SPRING

SIDE SCALE

END PIN

SHIELD

CENTER PIN

MARK SIDE COVER

BOLSTER

END PIN

POCKET KNIFE MEASUREMENTS

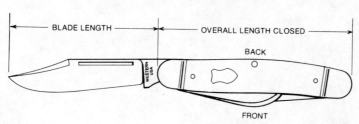

BLADE LENGTH

OVERALL LENGTH CLOSED

BACK

FRONT

NOTE: On all measurements allow dimensional tolerances for hand work.

NOTE: All terminology is as used by Western Cutlery. Most terms and spellings are traditional in the knife industry and may not be found in dictionaries.

Chart II - Pocket and Folding Knives

This drawing, copyright © 1975 by Western Cutlery Co., clearly defines the major terms involved in discussing folding knife features and construction.

19

Knife Design

3 If the blade is thick — 3/16-inch stock or more — the knife is a reshaped weapon. Knives as tools are mostly made of thin stock. Most American belt knives demonstrate their dagger beginnings.

There's a whole list of reasons for this, of course. Belt knives, as often as not, are carried as all-purpose instruments. I have used a belt knife to pry open the window of my own car; a friend of mine was once stuck on a rock face, one extra step from safety, and a stout knife stuck into a crack gave him the extra step; a heavy-bladed knife can both chop and cut. I know three fellows who have been attacked by large dogs and killed them with belt knives. I also know a fellow who did one with his bare hands, and he was rarely without a knife thereafter. Most belt knives are carried because these dramatic sorts of things do happen. The knife really need be only handy enough to cut string, rough-dress game animals, and slice salami; it *must* be stout enough to provide reasonable confidence it won't break in an above-average crunch.

American designers early on got clever at combining basic strength without awkwardness. Before the Bowie, there were so-called "rifle" knives—really thrusting weapons—that a fellow could gralloch with if he practiced. And men carried daggers as weapons, pure and simple — there were no reliable repeating handguns—and butchered game with pocketknives or regular butcher tools. I have seen an 1830s rifle bag, all original, with a slim 5-inch dagger sheathed on its shoulder strap.

While the Colt was making its way into American life, the Bowie or other large knife was a sidearm. When the sidearm of choice became a revolving pistol during the War Between the States, knife makers shrank the Bowie to six inches or so and the basic American hunting knife was born.

Since then there have been only refinements — shorter, longer, wider, narrower, more straight edge, more curve, higher point, lower point, thinner, thicker, guarded, guardless, straight grip, curved grip, shaped grip—back and forth the designs have gone.

There is no best design. There are only best designs for: for certain people, for certain jobs, for certain demands.

The world around, primitive peoples do the same things with knives. They perform camp chores, butcher small and large game, prepare food and fibers, work with hides, and the knife shapes they use vary as widely as their skin colors and physiques. In Finland, there are basically two knife-using peoples — Finns and Lapps—and two knife shapes. Finns carry the narrow-pointed *puuko*; the Lapp knife is broad bladed and wide at the tip. Obviously, since they are in the same land, both styles must work on some of the same jobs.

The sickle, with its edge on the inside curve, and the half-round *ooloo* of the Eskimos, with its edge on the outside curve, are the two extremes possible. From one all the way around to the other, all the shapes have been tried. The crooked skinner of North

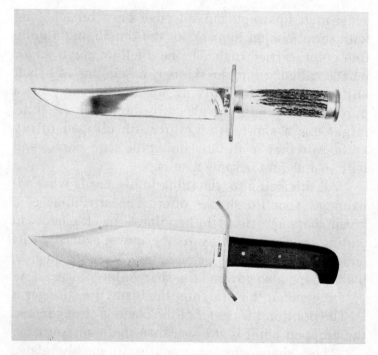

These two nineteenth-century-style big knives are types of Bowies. Both are modern made, but the blade size —over 8 inches —and shape make them Bowies nonetheless. The top one is a W-K hand-made specimen, the lower a Western Cutlery standard model. Altered somewhat and shrunk, these shapes became the typical modern American belt knife.

America, for instance, has almost the same shape as the Nepalese *kukri*, but the edges are on opposite sides.

Some time ago this writer came to the conclusion that for most North American belt use, a knife 4 to 5 inches long with a medium point, some straight edge, and some curve would do, and any knife that offered all of those with not too thick a blade was OK. That point of view simply realizes there is no perfect shape. Equally, there is no imperfect shape.

Of course, for any one user and for his uses, there are best shapes. A standard design will work for most jobs, but a knife is only an extension of a hand, so that hand has something to say in the matter. It is all very well for all Finns to be suited by a short, narrow saber-ground blade with a sharp, slightly lifted point, no guard, and a plain wood handle. American citizens will have no such regimentation.

One fellow likes the old Marble's Woodcraft pattern—a short knobbed handle with a single guard and a 4½-inch upswept, curved edge on a broad blade with serrations on its back for the thumb and a quite fine point, carried high. The next fellow might go for what's called a buffalo skinner, a scimitar of a belt knife with an edge curving up all the way and a purchase for the thumb ahead of the handle. A third might use a short, straightforward, clipped utility knife. And they're all three doing the same chores and with just about the same results.

All this being so, the thing to discuss is what advantages specific shapes offer. The attributes of a given shape are strength, handiness, or efficiency, in cutting, and adaptability to the owner's needs. The latter two are not the same thing. To some degree, blade shape also governs the sharpening process.

In general, the straighter the blade the stronger it is. The point in the center of the blade is stronger, and the dropped point is stronger than the high point.

These shape-affected strengths are mostly related to twisting efforts. There's a bit of a paradox, of course, since a wide blade is stronger than a narrower blade of the same stock. However, if the broad blade sticks its point too high, then the leverage can break it off.

The trade-off, naturally, is that a fine point is most useful, and a very stout point is not, obviously, very fine. There is, as another trade-off, a lot of use in a sweeping curved edge as opposed to a straight edge. And so that argument goes.

Today, you can get a Bowie design from 5 to 16 inches, so possibly that specific shape is worth discussing. For the record, there is considerable controversy among the very knowledgeable about the true Bowie shape, which means "What did the actual knife carried by Jim Bowie look like?" There are several possibilities, among them a spear point and a single edge with straight back. However, the front runner is a broad clip blade with false edge sharpened (in "serious" knives), double guarded, and heavily con-

structed. The clip provides, in most examples, a con-vex curve from the back to a slightly upswept point that is very nearly in the center of the blade. Such a knife balances forward, but is not so point-heavy as it would be without the clipped point. If it has a fault as a design, it is in the point, which is not nearly as sturdy as the rest of the knife. This is particularly true in lightweight Bowie types.

One advantage of the clipped-point Bowie shape, in paradox, is that it does offer a fine point at the end of a large blade. The very stout spear point is rarely fine enough for any reasonably delicate work unless the knife is slimmed down considerably, almost to penknife size.

There are plenty of belt-knife designs in the stores. If you can't find something close to your heart's desire in a cutlery department, you haven't looked hard enough.

25

In all, point preferences have to be developed in use. In general, I find a sharp point to be more useful than it is annoying. Where that point is makes more difference. There is, right now, a considerable vogue among writers and custom knife makers for the dropped point, at least partly as a reflection of twentieth-century hunting practice. The function for which most belt knives are carried is dressing-out game, yet we no longer do the whole job on larger game.

Most hunters field-dress only. That is, they open the animal enough to get the insides to the outside. They don't skin and they don't bone and they don't butcher. Perhaps the most practiced men in the country at gutting whitetail deer are the fellows who guide hunters at the YO Ranch in Texas. The ranch is deer heaven and is managed to keep it that way. The hunting, therefore, is fairly simple. The upshot is that a YO guide may dress two to eight deer almost every day of the season.

The exercise is a marvel of skill. With a deer down, the guide drives his vehicle as close as he can. He dismounts and, after suitable conversation, rolls the carcass over and the knife work starts. Parting the belly hair, he cuts through the abdominal wall from the ribs to the pelvis, running the knife inside and cutting outwards. He then runs the knife in alongside the anus and cuts all around, then reaches inside and pulls the whole gut in, clearing the pelvic cavity.

Here is where it gets stunty. He steps over the deer, one foot or both on a hind leg, runs his knife inside the pelvis and rips the bone open with an up-cut. He then turns around and, in the case of a deer that won't be mounted, uses the knife to rip up through the sternum and then all the ribs. This takes a stout knife and a stout edge.

For a head mount, the YO guide rips part way; then skins the chest out—leaving it loose but in place —and rips a few more ribs, then proceeds. (Some just

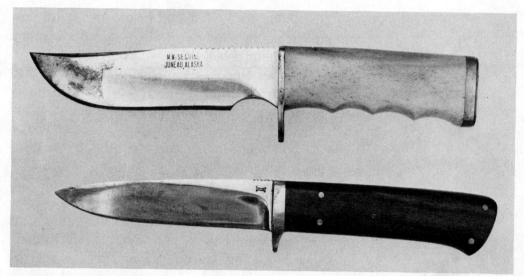

do the remaining work by reaching up into the chest cavity.) With the deer open from chin to tail, he reaches in and cuts the moorings of the diaphragm and the esophagus and windpipe and other stuff and tugs it all loose. Then, maybe with some help, he lifts the deer and turns it over. The guts all fall on the ground and he humps the carcass into the big iron basket on his vehicle's bumper, where it will drain nicely. Unless you say something, most of them leave the heart and liver right in the gut pile.

The Seguine handmade knife (top) follows, with minor changes, the short Bowie prescription. The Ralph Bone knife below it, however, is what is called a dropped-point hunter these days. Dropping the point makes, many feel, a better design for gutting and field-dressing game animals.

I have never seen one of these fellows in a hurry. The several times I have seen them do this, it takes maybe five minutes and you're hunting again.

What sort of knife do they use? Well, they run longer than average and stouter than average. There is a custom knife maker named Fisher who has a YO Special designed for the job I've just described. It is heavy and long with a 6- or 7-inch almost-straight blade and definite dropped point, but not too wide, perhaps 1½ inches at the guard and tapering from there. Apart from an ability to hold a good edge, a knife used in such specialized fashion should be big enough to lean on and if its point is out of the way, that helps for speed.

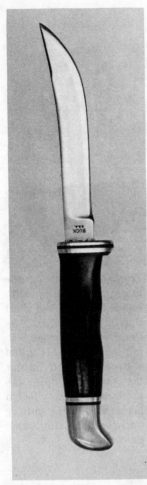

This is the Buck Personal; it is almost unique in the market as a slender curved belt knife, offering light weight and cutting efficiency if you want and can use the curve.

YO guides don't all spend heavy money for custom knives, not by a long shot. They are working men. A good commercial belt knife—Case, Western, Kabar, Schrade are all fine — 4½ inches or longer of 3/16 stock, does for most of them. You won't find many with raised points, however. Most are straight utility blades with clipped points. Cowboys being cowboys, there are no doubt some out there getting the job done with pocketknives.

Of course, there are lots of ways to gut deer. And a few deer hunters need to save minutes when the hunt is over. That's the point for the YO guide — his day isn't over until dark, and more happy hunters equals more money. He hunts two dudes at a time, and one deer on the ground equals one dude hot to go get his right now. Two deer on the ground means head for the barn for fresh dudes. If he draws good shooters all day, and the weather is right, a YO guide can put eight deer down between sunup and sunset and not overwork himself.

That fellow's knife works hard in the field, but he doesn't use it on anything but fresh carcasses. There's another batch of employees who skin and quarter the carcasses to go home with the dudes, or go to the locker plant. They use butchering implements.

Many deer hunters function the same way. They gut the deer and the locker plant does the rest. And that's why the dropped point is popular — you can open the abdomen and keep the point out of the guts pretty easily. You don't have to get very far into skinning a deer, however, to discover the dropped point, if it is at all sharp, is in just the wrong place. If you're punching the skin off a hanging deer, you find you have to keep your hand below the cut. This is particularly true if your knife is 6 inches long. The knife is wrong for the chore.

A different blade, with curve in the edge, lets you sweep the cut along and, as you rock your hand toward the end, the point fades up and away from the cut, slicing its way out. The dropped point seems to get stuck in the work because you run out of edge, and so to finish a long cut, you have to make a fresh start.

Understand that you can have both the dropped point and suitability for skinning and slicing. You get the latter with plenty of belly in the edge—it curves—so you can keep the slice going by rocking your hand. However, and here's another trade off, the only way to get the required belly into the edge is by making it wider. The blade can get too broad, and it gets difficult to work in tight spots or to make small cuts. That explains why the dropped-point design is not yet a big item in commercial hunting knives. The nearest they get is the regular straight clipped blade, which in truth is close enough for the work.

The commercial catalogs are full of knives offering long curved edges, most often with broad blades. The reason is that if you're slicing — or cutting in a slicing motion, as with skinning — you can start the cut close to your hand if you have a curved edge, and you can keep the cut going deep or long. If your 5-inch blade has 3 inches of straight edge, you just have 2 inches of curve to play with.

The chosen shape depends on where the user wants his power, and where he wants his slice to start. A knife is used to slice, whether it be little cuts or long cuts, by pulling it across the work while pressing the edge into the work, or as a sort of horizontal chisel, by those who have found a sharp edge and the quick application of muscle work best for them. When the straight chiseling action doesn't work, sawing the blade back and forth combines the slash or slice with the chisel effect.

Wherever you see a man slashing instead of sawing, and slicing instead of chiseling crossways, you see quicker, neater work. Whatever shape lets you do that in the work you actually do—and we'll take, for the moment, as given that there is a good edge, a good

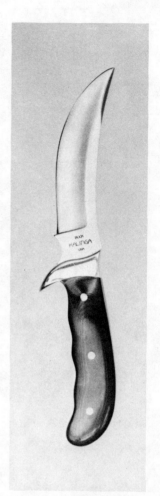

Buck has another curved knife, the deluxe Kalinga. This is a heavy-duty knife with pretty good looks.

handle, and the right relationship between the two—is the shape for you.

My own most-used belt knives offer as much curve as straight, and a slightly high point doesn't bother me, either. I simply don't gut enough deer in a big hurry to give away the advantages of a narrower blade with curve in it.

The answer might well be a knife with a narrow curved blade. You get the curved edge, the fine high point, the light weight all at once. No such blade is on the commercial market, except the Buck Personal. That knife is called the Personal because it was apparently the chosen carrying knife of H. H. Buck, whose family still owns the knife company of the same name. It is a useful knife and does everything we're discussing here — provide sweeping cuts, get into nooks and crannies easily, cut stuff like leather in reasonably small radii—but, and it is a big but, you have to relearn how to do a lot of cutting you're used to doing with a straighter blade. You don't get power at the point with a curved narrow blade. It cuts, but it doesn't poke well.

The discussion can spin on forever, but it cannot escape the basic truth that the user is the key. A good knife man with a single-edged razor blade might well outperform a bumbler with a rack of superior blades. For every one of us there is a general shape and size that suits our general need, but only we can find it.

The Shape You Want

4 Shape depends, as they say, on the situation and the terrain. However, there are some ground rules.

The first question to answer concerning the shape of the belt knife you should carry is whether you carry a pocketknife. If you do, then its smaller blades will be available for fine cutting and you can pick the belt model for stunts it can pull off that the little blade can't touch. The second question concerns weight. For 6 or 8 ounces, you can carry quite a big blade, but half a pound is definitely noticeable on the belt. So is 8 inches of blade, which means at least a foot of knife.

The Bowie shape works fine at short lengths. As the classic double guard would get in the way, it is usually replaced with a single short guard, and the sharpened false edge, annoying in a work knife, is generally dropped. For the rest of it, you get some straight edge and some curve and a fine point. Moreover, the basic Bowie broad blade can be and is narrowed; it can be and is left broad, but shortened; the clip may be straightened out for strength — there are a lot of derivatives of the Bowie, and most of them work.

There are also other basic shapes that are as "American" as the Bowie. One of these is the plain spear point, where the back curves to meet the edge at a point near the centerline of the blade. Collectors call robust nineteenth-century specimens of this style "Rio Grande Camp Knives" when they are broad bladed and 6 inches long or longer. The main blade on most Boy Scout knives is a fair rendering of this shape.

Such a shape is strong. The point, of course, is not fine, and there is not much curve in the edge. This is a "utility" shape, not set up primarily for gutting and skinning game animals. It will serve, of course, particularly if it is thin in the blade and hollow ground. For slicing bread and bologna, making shavings and kindling, trimming meat and peeling potatoes, it works.

In Scandinavia they favor slim short blades with slightly raised points. Mostly saber ground, such *puuko* (in Finnish and similar in other tongues) blades are strong and handy. At 3 inches in length, and shorthandled, such a knife works like a sharp finger; at greater length, it will handle a wide variety of jobs. Much over 5 inches, the Finnish shape becomes a knife particularly suited to fishermen's chores.

Butchers' tools have lent their shapes to belt knives. Boning knives, skinning knives, and the common bluntly pointed butcher knife can all be found made of thick stock, with guards and fancy handles. One old American shape, typified in the Marble's Woodcraft model of yore, is simply a sheep skinner with the top of the blade clipped. There's no straight edge at all on this shape. The edge sweeps in an upward curve from guard to point, and the point is high and quite fine. It's a useful shape.

Inventive fellows occasionally conceive different shapes that seem to work. The Russell belt knife, of Canadian origin, puts a leaf-shaped blade together with an offset handle that angles up from the blade.

These shapes are rather special, which figures since they are not commercial knives, but Randalls. The second, third, and fourth from the top are somewhat general-purpose knife blades. The others are what one fellow or another came up with as the ideal knife for him, and Randall decided to see if others would like them. Commercial firms cannot, of course, afford to indulge their fancies this way.

Here are a couple more commercial knives — Schrade at right, Case at left —that take the middle of the road. The Case is really a long, thin Finn. Either will do the work.

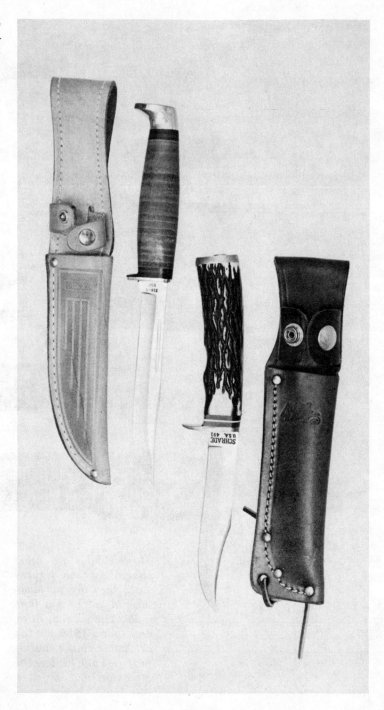

The result is spear point strength with a curved cutting edge all well below the knuckles. The knife tends to be a little wedgy, but that is not necessarily a fault in a belt knife.

In many hunting places of the world, long custom decrees what the hunter and outdoorsman wear for cutlery. In North America, however, anything goes. There is some Finn, some German, some Latin, some Scot, some of everywhere in all of us. In sportsmen's cutlery there are no rules, no dictates of fashion or custom. Since it really doesn't make all that much difference anyway and a fellow could learn to use anything from a sickle to a pizza wheel, the choice boils down more to a question of materials and workmanship than to shape and style. Any good knife will do, so use what you like and use it well.

The question of blade length comes up when you talk about shape. To some degree, the question is academic since all shapes and types are not available at all lengths. If you're determined on a given shape, say a Finnish, you'll search a long time for one longer than 5 inches, unless you get a fish knife.

People are fond of saying that the real experts carry short knives, the implication being that a guy with a longish knife is a klutz. That just is not so. There are several ways to look at the question: One is that you probably keep a pocketknife around for short-blade chores, so you can get whatever benefit a long blade affords for no penalty in handiness. Another is that there are marked benefits in a long-bladed belt knife. When they get out to 7 or 8 inches, certain sorts of work get easy. There was a time, for instance, when an 8-inch Western Cutlery belt knife was part of my turkey-hunting kit, because with it I could cut a bunch of palmetto fronds in a hurry to make blinds. You get dingle hooks and toasting sticks quicker with the big blade. And if you're killing and butchering big animals, the work goes more quickly with the big ones.

This is an Americanized Finn with a 3-inch blade. I'd consider it small for dealing with deer, but hard to beat for smaller game.

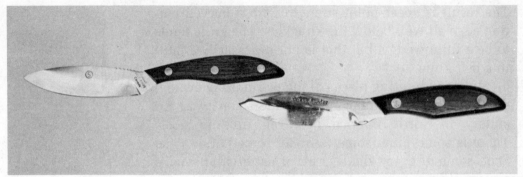

Once in a while someone comes up with variation enough to be called new, and the Russell Belt Knife at left is one such. It is very different in the hand from the knife at right, which is labeled "Yukon Hunter" and cannot be considered a good copy. It's a lot clumsier.

There's a knife-making friend of mine who used to hunt deer in the Cumberland Gap country. At the time he favored an 11-inch knife, made of ⅛ or thinner stock — one of his own, of course. This one year they were killing deer real well, and they were kidding my blacksmith friend about his knife pretty good also. There came the day when there were eight fresh deer in a pickup. There was a challenge, and a deer-skinning and quartering contest ensued. The best man with the knife among the kidders used a little 4-inch experts knife.

Here's how my friend describes the result: "He beat me skinning, but I finished my four first."

In detail, the skilled man using the short knife like a finger can get the skin off a deer in handy fashion while the man operating the big blade is at a disadvantage. Then, the shoe moves to the other foot with all that meat to cut. The big knife goes through in one slash while the shorty has to make the same cut three or four times.

How long is long? Well, in general a 5-inch knife is in the middle. A 3-inch blade is definitely short; a 4-incher is pretty short. A 6-incher is a little long and 7 inches and more are definitely long knives.

Personally, I tend to use 5-inch knives, not too curved, not too straight. So I think it's hard to go wrong with a 5-incher. That's long enough for a lot of work and short enough that I don't have to explain why I like it. But the 3½ and 3-inch knives are better

From P Ashley Cooper
Governor of The Hudson's Bay Company.
1934

for dressing small game and birds, and to gut fish as you catch them. And they'll do for deer. At 4 and 4½ inches there is enough edge to make good long cuts. Some of the custom makers standardize hunters' designs at 4 inches and design their shapes around it.

The 5-inch knife has mostly general-purpose advantages over 4-inch blades. You can slice bread with a 5-incher, for instance, quite handily. I find it a useful extra inch.

At 6 inches, you have more of the same. The edge is getting long enough for big strokes and the weight is there, too. However, the sheathed 6-inch knife is getting up toward 12 inches long overall. There are longer belt knives for sportsmen, but not many. Beyond 6 and 7 inches you're getting into multipurpose tools and weapons. Still, for long decades—even centuries — the standard belt knives were big, and people managed, despite the reputed unhandiness of the long blade.

What it comes down to is that the choice of belt knife is very personal and you should get the length

Knives of this general shape —about 4½ inches in the blade —have been much used in the North Country. This one was given to a man I met by the Governor of the Hudson's Bay Company back in the 1930s and later rehandled by the great knife maker Scagel. It's been many a mile and made many a cut in the woods.

Here is a late entry in the North-Country knife-design stakes: It's not so different, except that Randall has added a straight chopping edge to the back of the blade.

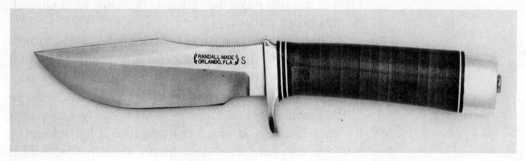

RANDALL MADE
ORLANDO, FLA. S

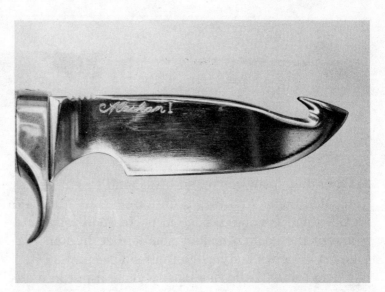

This is a gut hook. It costs extra and it's not worth it, in my opinion. If you must have one, see that it is sharp only back in the curve; a sharp point is unnecessary and dangerous. You don't stick the point of the hook in and unzip. You use the knife point to make a slit and then introduce the hook.

you like. After all, if you're wrong, you can always get another knife. Everyone needs a spare knife.

There are some special design features on the market worth talking about. One of these is the gut hook, a special-purpose hook ground into the back of the knife. Some people grind them into their own commercial knives. The purpose is to turn the upside-down eelly cut into a simple zipper stroke: You make a small cut, introduce the hook, and zip open the abdomen.

I don't like the gut hook. It is like having a second sharp edge and I know that if I carried one as a habit, I would, sooner or later, zip open the sheath or my clothes or even my own skin. Opening up an animal has never been so difficult or time consuming for me. I freely admit I have never tried the hook long enough to find other virtues.

There is a vogue right now for fat knives, knives with very wide short blades. The idea seems to be that much heavy-duty knife work is encountered by people who don't carry personal hatchets. In the custom-knife business, smoke jumpers were early customers for such designs. It is a fact that given a hefty handle, a fellow can lean hard on a heavy short blade. And it

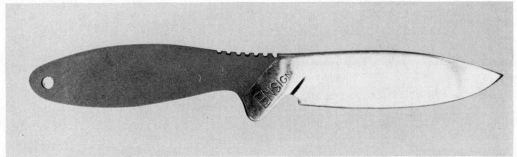

is another fact that the right short design can handle nearly everything but slicing.

There are also what might be called skeletonized knives on the market. They are one-piece stainless steel, and look terribly modern. The handle is a simple steel outline. These knives are mostly cast, not ground and machined, although there may be some fellow who wastes his time chopping them from the solid. The casting is doubtless cleaned up on wire wheels and buffers and the edges are ground, but otherwise the knives are made at one pass. They are nevertheless pretty good knives. Some friends took a batch of them to Africa on safari and they worked well with no failures. Some of these blades look radical—one is nothing more nor less than a quarter circle with the edge on the circumference—but they are actually well thought out and quite functional.

There have begun to be knives offered with handles shaped for the individual fingers or with what have to be called subhilts. A small subhilt on a knife I thought I might have to fight with might be OK, and a shape that places the index finger likewise. I just won't fool with the rest of it. I do like a place to put my finger ahead of the guard for when I shorten up, and this also makes the whole edge easier to sharpen.

No knife solves all the design problems, but it is a lot of fun to keep trying for that perfect—for you—knife.

This Ensign knife may be machined from the bar, but many such knives are cast. That doesn't matter, incidentally, because if they are designed right and cast right, they're OK. But: a cast knife should be cheaper. There are models —made by Bowen among others —that have skeleton grips and also somewhat radical blade shapes that work well.

Knives For Your Pocket

5 Most of us have our pockets with us all the time and one of those pockets should have a knife in it. That's so even if there's a knife on your belt.

We'll make a distinction here between pocketknives and the large lock-blade folding hunters discussed in the next chapter. The lines between blur because there is much overlap in size and style. Here we're discussing only knives small enough or light enough for the pocket.

That gives us plenty to talk about. There are thousands of variations, hundreds of combinations, and scores of basic types. There were Roman pocket-size folding knives; colonial American pocketknives; and, when mass production arrived in the nineteenth century, there followed an explosion of cutlers' catalogs.

There is a way to tell whether or not the specific knife you're looking at is a good possibility, and this eliminates some uncertainty when the time comes to choose a pocketknife. There is no way to tell how a given blade size and shape will suit you until you've

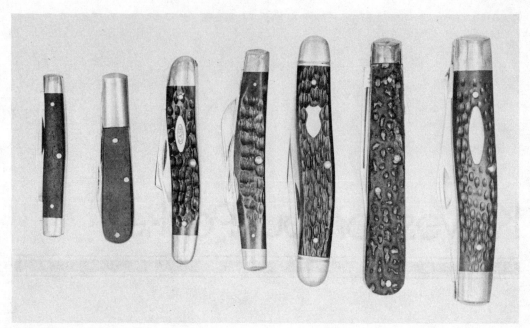

This is about the range of sizes in comfortable and useful pocketknives. The penknife at left is 2½ inches long; the double-ended jack at right, 4½ inches. The range is not at all complete, of course. There's probably a common model —or several — for every ⅛-inch difference between the two extremes.

tried it, and that goes double, of course, for a two-bladed knife. But quality in a pocketknife is always revealed by fit and finish in standard construction.

Fit means that the scales lay flat all around, butting tightly and evenly against the bolsters. Along the back of the knife, the five to nine separate layers of steel, brass, and—mostly, these days—plastic snuggle close to each other. The blades lie right where they should, sometimes on a little slant to let them nestle tight. No points stick out, and nail nicks are easy to get at.

The old language for fitting up blades says that a good knife walks and talks. That means that the blades come up halfway and hesitate, then snap open and will close the same way. The smooth opening with a stop if you want is "walking," and the click of the opening and closing is "talking."

Getting a knife to walk and talk takes careful assembly and a couple of special files, once the parts are properly made. The rear end of the blade bears on a spring, of course. As the blade is rotated from shut to open, the spring is flexed in a camming action. The hesitation, halfway open, is caused by a flat spot; tipped past the flat, the blade snaps open (or shut).

Given that the spring tension and blade-cam configuration are OK, the next problem is to make the blade shut properly, with its point down inside and, at the same time, have it point straight ahead when opened. The blade's height in its slot when closed is governed by a little pad of metal left on the blade just to the rear of the edge. How straight the knife will point is handled by the front end of the spring. The fitter simply files one and then the other spot, lowering the blade into the handle and raising the point into line.

Now, the trick is to do this for two, three, and four blades at a time and do it quickly enough to show a profit. It can be done, so you shouldn't settle for less. Don't buy a knife that doesn't walk and talk and line up to suit you.

Finish is the next thing to check out and, if the knife is a good one, its quality is easy to see because the knife is shiny. The ground-down parts of the scales are shiny, the bolsters are shiny, the blades are shiny, and a really first-class knife will shine like a mirror deep down inside — even the bottom of the springs. The shine goes all the way around every part of the knife. Polishing all those parts costs money.

However, there are some pretty good knives around that aren't shiny. The world being what it is, some firms held down prices by leaving out some of the traditional details. Obviously, finish is better skimped than fit. In this respect, price can be your guide. A knife with a clean, but not shiny, interior and plain-ground or dull-polished blades ought to be priced at least a couple of dollars under the same size and type in the full-finished category. And when it isn't, one of the knives is lying.

Quality levels based on finish have been around for some time. At the turn of the century, the Sears,

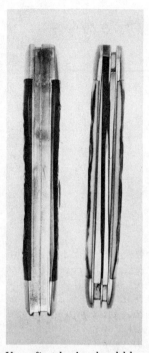

Your first looks should be at the back to check fit and finish, which is about perfect here; then inspect the closed blades closely. They're supposed to lie at angles to each other as in this specimen.

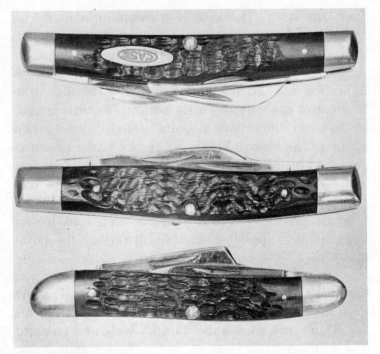

Roebuck catalog was very frank about them. On one of several pages devoted to knives, thirty models are shown. Those that cost 23¢ to 40¢ are steel lined, and no mention is made of finish; depending on the size, 45-centers are "finished throughout"; 55- and 60-centers are "highly finished throughout"; better knives are "finely finished in every detail"; the $1.25 and up models have "beautifully crocus polished blades," "satin finish throughout," and "excell all others in finish." Those differences are with us today, in about the same proportion. You may find that prices have gone up somewhat, of course.

Unfortunately, the temper and toughness of the blades are not so easily examined as the rest of the knife. The probability is that the better-finished knife will have the better-using blade, but another probability is that there will be a difference between one knife and its twin. And that leads to the likelihood, or even the certainty, that a $4 knife can be found that will outperform a $7.50 knife from the same maker. There

44

has not yet been developed a reliable method for telling which is which in advance. If you do develop such a method, patent it and sell it to a knife company, because they'd really put it to use. Don't misunderstand: Nobody plans it this way. That is just how it happens in mass production. (One man I used to know tried to beat it by always demanding to see three or four knives and buying the sharpest.)

Price and fit and finish and steel quality are all important, but they don't create problems. The big problem with pocketknife selection is deciding which model you want. There are always dozens of patterns and sizes. Naturally, very few of us make up· our minds without prior experience. Out of a considerable examination of the knives available and the way people use them, I'd say the questions to answer in your own mind are:

What's the knife for? That is, what will you expect it to do and how will it be carried in what sort of clothes?

How much weight and bulk can you stand? That is, pocketknives come in sizes and you ought to pay some attention to this because a half inch can make a lot of difference—one way or the other—in a knife.

What patterns have worked for you before? That is, our hands get habits of their own, and "remember" how to do things. A familiar pattern helps. This works the other way, too, and unsuccessful patterns should be avoided.

Here's a specific example: A 210-pound man commutes to his office by car from a house in the suburbs where a wife, two little kids and a dog and cat live with him on a half-acre lot. He warms a chair most of the day, wearing shirt and tie and slacks and jacket, with shiny shoes and the whole business bit.

What might his most-carried pocketknife look like? It's a 3 9/16-inch Schrade-Walden, Uncle Henry-quality, round-bolster stock knife in stainless steel. The three blades are: a California long clip at 2

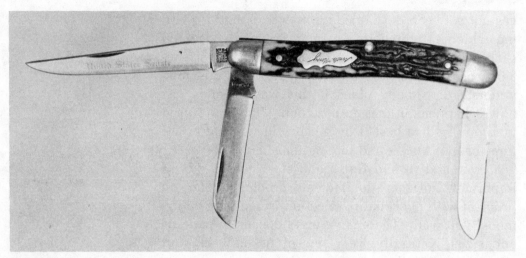

3/4 inches; a 2-inch sheepsfoot with straight edge; and a 2-inch spey blade. Some call that clip blade a skinning blade.

What are this knife's main jobs? Everyday, it cleans and scrapes a pipe, opens sundry envelopes, clips newspapers, cuts string, cuts rubber bands off a little girl's braids, cleans fingernails, and whittles a little. Often it is used to slice quick snacks off anything in the refrigerator, trim fat off a steak (rarely) or roast, and open bags of dog food or cardboard boxes. It picks slivers out of the flesh of children and roses off those bushes still alive. And sometimes it goes to work in a restaurant, which is funny but efficient, since some restaurants don't serve sharp knives.

How did he pick this particular knife? By unconsciously comparing it to a dozen others in use and discovering after a while that when he wasn't thinking about it, that's the one he picked up and put in his pocket.

What were the other knives? Four other stockmen's knives, all either larger or smaller with square bolsters; a small round-ended Boy Scout knife; a double-ended jackknife with large and small spear blades and pocket-saving canoe shape; a 4¼-inch lock-blade knife; a 4½-inch one-bladed jackknife; a

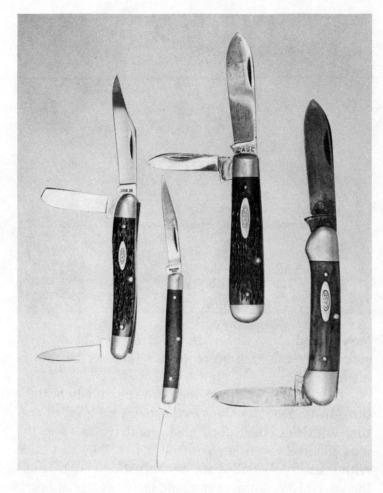

From the left, these may be described as a three-bladed stock knife, or just stock knife; a penknife; a jackknife; a double-ended jackknife. A penknife has a blade at each end, strictly speaking, while a jackknife has its blades at the same end. Large penknives are really double-ended jacks. You can also say of these (from the left) that they have master clip-spey-pen blades; master clip-pen blades; and master spear-pen fits both of the others. The master is, of course, the largest blade.

nice flat gardener's knife with genuine stag handle, a hawkbill, and a short spey blade; and a two-bladed muskrat knife offering identical long clip blades. And there were more. None of these knives, with the possible exception of the hawkbill blade on the gardening knife, fell short as an all-purpose knife. All had good metal, proper fit and function, and would sharpen nicely. But after a long while, they fell by the wayside in favor of the Schrade Uncle Henry.

I'm the guy, of course, and I find that one knife big enough for daily cutting and small enough for a business suit. The blade shapes fit what I do with a knife and I find the extra-slim, long clip blade particu-

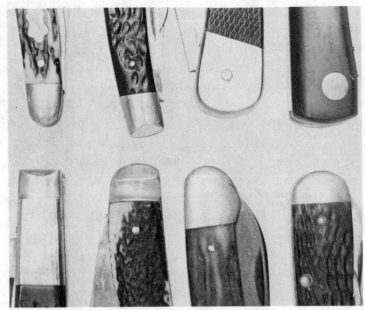

All of these have pocket-busting features. Square bolsters and blade corners sticking out are not overly kind to fabrics. A pocket-knife, if you're to get use out of it, is wearing out your pocket every waking moment of your life.

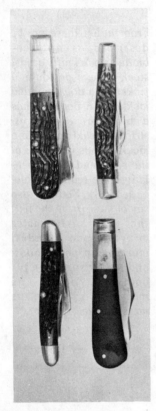

larly useful. Now that I think of it, that blade is to some degree a miniature of my favorite belt-knife blades.

Cowboys I've known keep the spey blade of their three-bladed stock knives extra sharp, do a lot of cutting with the sheepsfoot blade, and try to keep the long blade away from hard objects so they can slice with it nicely. I don't work my knife that way because the spey blade is the best shape to clean a pipe bowl, which dulls any knife. I keep the sheepsfoot very sharp, the long blade almost as sharp and use the spey a lot on rough cuts.

That's a lot of detail about a single knife with a single multifunction, but it does provide a starting point. At 3 9/16 inches and with three blades, it's about as middle-of-the-road as it can be. In conventional knives, a 2½-inch model is about as small as remains useful, and I have one that weighs ¾ of an ounce. For steady pocket wear, and to use, as it were, in public, 4 ¾ inches and 4 ounces has been my upper limit thus far. Whichever size is selected, it may be packaged as a jackknife, with one or two blades

48

pinned at the same end, or as a penknife, with blades pinned at opposite ends, or as that semantic anomaly, the double-ended jackknife. It can be square or rounded on the ends; rectangular, S-shaped, big-ended, or banana-shaped. Flat is nice, but thick is comfortable. There are reasons for all these shapes, but they are lost in their nineteenth-century origins. It makes more sense to discuss them pro and con.

The square-bolstered knives do good work, and for certain kinds of work with some blades the positive feel of what becomes the square shank on a cutting tool is worthwhile. But they wear pockets and they gouge.

The rounded bolsters, particularly the blunt ones, avoid the gouges and much of the pocket wear. There are some designs with swelled bolsters — oversize — to hide the sharp blade butts that wear pockets. The best known of these is a Case double-jack (just too large to be a penknife) called the Canoe. Every corner and rough edge is neatly tucked away when the knife is closed.

Shape counts, too. Very few knives are symmetrical in profile. They come with big butts and big heads — the shape's the same but reversed. You can get the slim part of the handle in your hand; you can have it the other way around. They come in the S-shape

Some designs furnish a master blade at the big end, some at the little. If you've never noticed, it could still make a difference to you. There are also equal-ended knives, but they're boring.

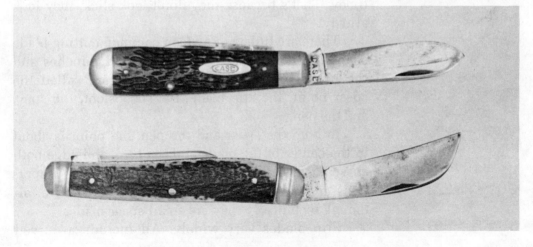

Here are the five principal blade shapes, and one oddball. From the top, these are clip, spear, spey, sheepsfoot, and pen blades. The one at the bottom, very uncomplicated, I call the plain blade. There doesn't seem to be a name for this shape.

called serpentine. In this one, you get one end that sits high and one low. It works pretty well. There are equal-end knives around. Most look somewhat old-timey. That's because they don't look slick; they look sturdy.

There are fifteen or sixteen common cutting-blade shapes, not counting screwdrivers and punches and the like. The five most-used shapes are called the spear point, the clip blade, the sheepsfoot, the spey, and the pen.

In both the spear and the pen, the point is about in the center of the blade and the back and edge both curve to meet it. Pen blades have narrower proportions and finer lines and merit their own name, although technically they are small spear blades.

Clip blades vary widely. All include a curved

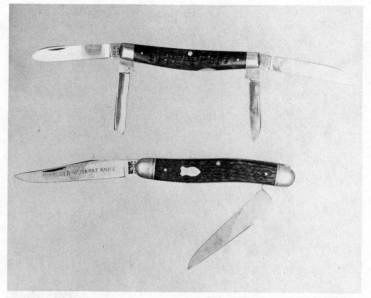

edge with the back slanting down to it in a concave curve. The clip can be short and steep or long and gentle. A long one is called sometimes a California clip. There is also a straight clip, which means there's no curve in the line of the clip.

The sheepsfoot has a straight edge with the back brought down to it in a curve. This varies, so the sheepsfoot sometimes has a fine point. A heftier variation is called a Wharncliffe.

The spey blade is rather blunt up front—in fact, has a steep, short clip — and offers a curved edge. Spey blades are often rather thin and are good for delicate cutting.

Some combination of these five blades will manage most cutting jobs. They are therefore often combined in two- and three-bladed knives. Specific combinations in two-bladed knives are clip-pen, clip-sheepsfoot-pen, sheepsfoot-spey and spey-pen, the larger or master blade mentioned first. Three-bladed knives generally have a clip or spear as the large blade and a choice of the other three, as: clip-pen-sheepsfoot; clip-spey-sheepsfoot; clip-spey-pen; clip-pen-pen.

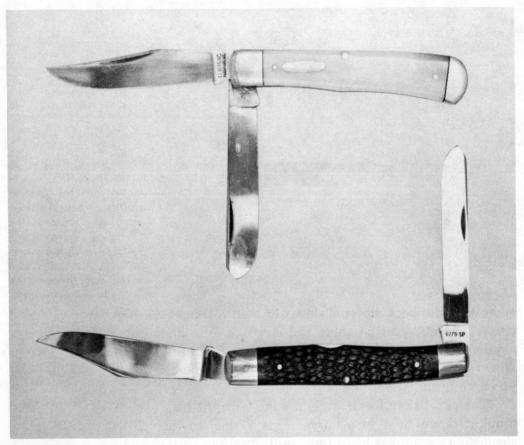

The upper knife is a trapper from L. L. Bean. The clip / long spey combination in this handle shape is always called a trapper — even the much lighter weight model you see around. The other knife, a Case, is not often seen, but it is, naturally, a double-ended trapper.

Some combinations are so traditional that knives that offer them have specific names. A 4-inch or larger two-bladed jackknife with a long clip blade and an equally long spey blade is a trapper model. The three-bladed combination of clip-spey-sheepsfoot is a stock or premium stock knife. A 4-inch knife in serpentine shape with an identical skinning or California clip blade at each end is a muskrat knife.

There are other cutting blades, most of them designed for specific kinds of work or function. The hawkbill is for pruning; the coping blade, a thin and small rectangular slip of steel, is for fine cuts in wood. The surgical lance or scalpel blade is slim and fine with a concave edge, good for splinters; there's a square-edged blade often used on boats. There's a razor blade, shaped like a straight razor, and a slim sheepsfoot. And there's what we'll call a plain blade because it has no name — it has a straight back and the edge simply curves up to it. There's a curved pruning blade that isn't hawkbill shaped; and the thin flat-ground California clip called a skinning blade, even though it looks nothing like a fixed-blade skinner, which has a markedly curved blade.

The addition of some of these blades to the more important ones creates yet more pocketknife styles with names of their own. A three-bladed knife with a master clip blade, a pen blade, and a coping blade is called a whittler. There is a congress penknife, a square-bolstered banana shape with the blades in the convex side, either a pen-pen or a pen-sheepsfoot combination. Add a large sheepsfoot and a coping blade to these and you get the four-bladed congressional whittler. A razor blade master in combination with one or two others is called, by some, the one-handed man's knife, since it can be opened one handed.

When you consider that virtually all the combinations come in several sizes overall, and that there are additional variations in the type of grind provided, things get complicated without even noting that there are slight to considerable differences between the different makers' renditions of the various shapes.

In the matter of grinds, there are three — saber grind, hollow grind and flat grind. In the saber grind, largely confined to clip blades, the blade blank is left full thickness for a third to a half of its width. The flat-ground knife has flat sides tapered from back to edge. More metal is ground away, making the flat sides concave, in the hollow grind. Some makers do a very slight hollow grind called whittening.

Somewhere in all of these shapes and sizes there is just the general-carrying pocketknife for you. Chances are you'll try a few before you settle down to

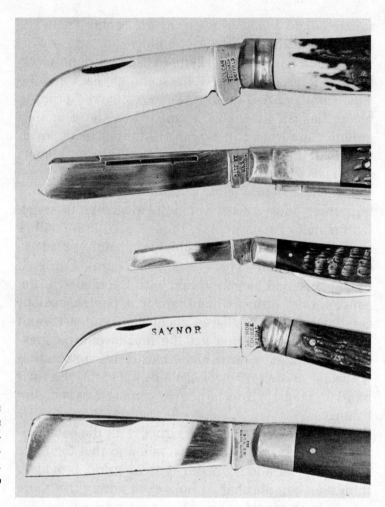

Here are some not-so-usual blade shapes, each with its own name. From the top, they are the hawkbill, razor, coping, pruning, and square-end. Those who get used to these swear by them.

one just about like the one your father or uncle used. Unless you're different from most of us, at least one of the blades on your chosen knife will have a fine point and you'll keep one blade for fine cutting; and when you get a good one, you'll brag about it.

All this problem of selection and choice wouldn't apply if you were Chinese. A friend who has spent a lot of time in touch with Chinese culture tells me there is a single design acceptable to the Chinese. Whatever the cutlers of the world do, the Chinese wants a broad, leaf-shaped blade with a curved minimum handle. The specimen I have has brass fit-

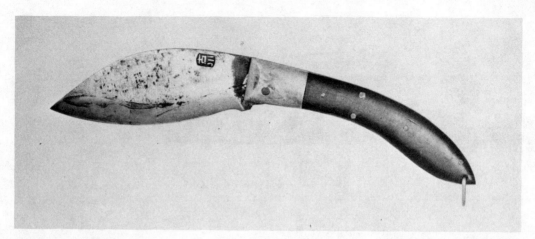

This knife — it folds — is the non pareil favorite of the Chinese and given any choice they'll have no other. To pile strangeness upon strangeness, it has a bevel edge. It would take me three months to get used to it.

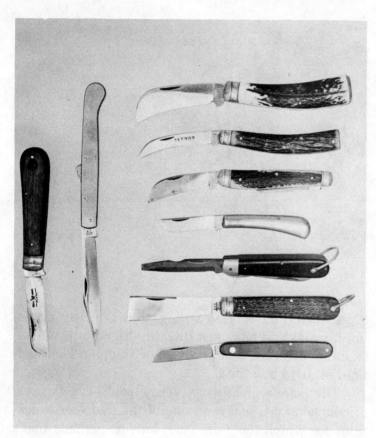

These knives are set up for specific kinds of jobs. At left is a very stout work knife —crate opening and all that —alongside a slim pocket carving knife, no less, from England. On the right, from the top, are three different gardener's knives; a nickel-silver-handled budding knife for gentleman orchardists; an electrician's knife; a pointless design for sailors and yachtsmen; and a folding bevel-edge patch knife used in muzzle-loader shooting.

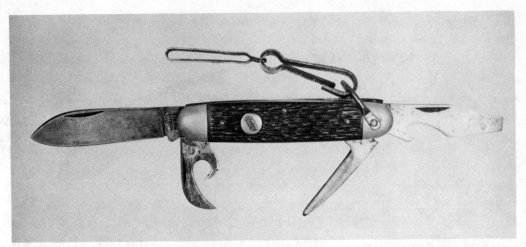

Here is a well-used and very typical Boy Scout knife, four blades, shackle and belt fitting, and all. The design has been set for decades. How much leather-punching we do anymore is debatable, but the generations who have known this design insist on it. In truth, the assembly is handy.

The Victorinox Camper model of the Swiss Army knife offers ten blades, plus toothpick (shown partly drawn at the saw-blade) and tweezers (lying atop the knife). The blades are, clockwise from the saw, cork-screw, small screwdriver-reamer, leather punch, large spear, can opener with screwdriver tip, scissors, caplifter/screw-driver, small pen blade, three-sided file. To get all this together just right — and this is a good one — takes money.

tings, including a brass spring, and is pretty crude, but it walks and talks just fine. My friend tells me the Chinese brush the best products of Solingen and Shef-field aside to buy these.

There are a great many specialized pocketknives, of course, and if you're in one of the trades or avoca-tions for which there are such knives, perhaps that's your choice. Probably the nearly universal avocation male Americans get exposed to first, which has — or had—its own knife is the Boy Scouts of America.

Say "utility combination knife" or "camper's knife" to the average fellow and he has to think about it. Say "Boy Scout knife" and he sees, instantly, an equal-ended, round-bolstered, four-bladed knife with a master spear blade, a leather punch, a cap-lifter/screwdriver, a can opener, and a lanyard shackle.

Such a design is so familiar to Americans and has such utility for them that the Boy Scout knife in all-metal style is an item of issue in all branches of the U.S. military service. It has been that way for three decades or so.

For the purist, this American utility knife is so general purpose it can be viewed as a little limited, particularly for the business of cutting. Still, it's an awfully handy item to have around, so much so that it has plenty of competition. There are dozens of approaches to the same problem. Chief among them is that vast family of utility knives known collectively as the Swiss Army knife. In point of fact, the Swiss Army issues—you guessed it—an equal-ended four-bladed knife with master spear blade, leather punch, cap-lifter/screwdriver, can opener, and shackle. It is all metal and they figured out a way to add a second and smaller screwdriver bit on the can opener, but otherwise, it's your good old Boy Scout knife.

The commercial Swiss Army knives are something else. There are many models. They are all done up very handsomely, with dense red plastic handles. The variety of blades is astounding and includes scissors, saws, metal files, and fish scalers, not to mention built-in tweezers and toothpicks. Such knives are staple items in the kits of people who travel a lot, and make sense for that.

There are other—and sometimes classier—utility knives to be found in cutlery stores. I have a six-blader by Henckels that is smaller than the typical Boy Scout knife — quite pocketable — which has the usual stuff plus a second cutting blade and a

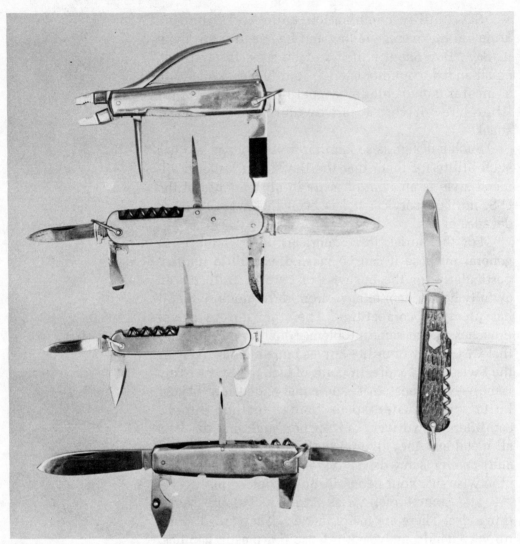

Other entries in the combination field are German and British and Italian. This collection, you'll note, sticks with the same old basics, the pliers model being the exception. The Sheffield-made IXL knife (second from top) is notably stout, and has nickel-silver handle scales. This model is known as an officer's knife. The Henckels model below it is notably compact. The stag-handled knife at right is probably a hunter model, offering only an awl, corkscrew, and screwdriver (at base of spear blade) besides the two cutting blades.

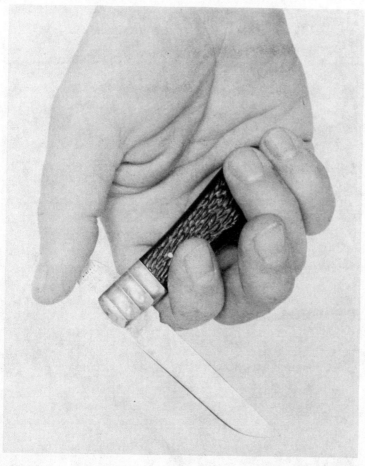

This one-hand model is opened by pulling a forward projection of the blade through 180°, hauling the blade out of the handle. With a different blade shape, I could have gotten a lot more interested in this one.

corkscrew. I have a bone-handled IXL with five blades that is a nice straightforward knife, and another IXL six-blader in all metal that is oversize, but a considerable knife. You can get a pocket mechanics' outfit with, so help me, built-in pliers. There is probably no end to it, but your basic four-bladed knife will do most of it.

There are special knives for gardeners. These usually include hawkbill or pruning blades and spey blades, the latter specialized for budding and grafting. And we all know about the Army's TL-29, the electricians' knife with a spear blade and a locking wire-stripper/screwdriver blade.

There are one-hand knives, with various patented

Three work knives are shown here—an extra-big 5-inch stock knife at top, a special Case design with several names, my favorite being "sunfish," and a sturdy American-made Schrade rope knife. The latter two are useful for heavy cutting jobs.

features for this and that apart from the typical blade construction adapted to one-handing it. There are, from foreign sources, pocket carving knives and from our own makers very similar fruit knives. The slim two-bladed fish knife that is equipped with a scaler/hook-disgorger/bottle-opener blade alongside a thin useful clip blade is a purely American type.

The Barlow knife is not a model of handle/blade configuration, but rather any jackknife with an ex-

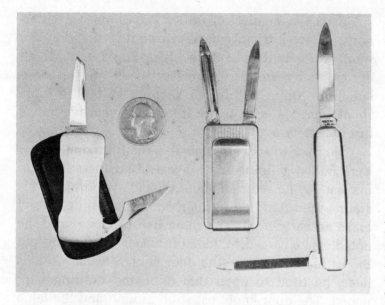

tended bolster. The idea was to beef up cheap knives, but it works on expensive knives, too.

There are small lock-blade knives in plentiful supply. They are simply one-bladed jackknives with extra security in use. The locking feature doesn't make much sense unless the whole knife is sturdy enough to lean on pretty hard. If it is, then the lock is a good idea.

We haven't discussed the exclusive territory of the small penknife, the gentleman's pocketknife, the, so help me again, executive knife. These exist in thousands of variations, and some of the most highly decorated, carefully worked knives ever made have been such. People give them away as souvenirs and incorporate them in money clips and miniaturize them past utility. The basic model incorporates a small pen blade for cutting string, and a fancy fingernail-cleaning file. To this is added a scissor, perhaps, which is somewhat better than no scissor at all, or a second cutting blade, or a measuring tape. In general, as sold today, these are knives for people who don't carry knives. I never bought one myself. I have some, but none of them are on purpose.

This complicated little machine is a yachtsman's special and if I were a yachtsman I'd pass along a few tips. That spike, I know, is a marlinspike, useful for splicing and unknotting ropes. Curiously, some armies still issue knives with marlinspikes —they still use ropes, not nylon straps and webbing. This knife is sold by Blackstone.

Even the smallest of utility knives are worth carrying. I have a friend whose constant companion is a small knife with a cutting blade, a scissors, of all things, and a small screwdriver blade. He has been heretofore quite faithful in keeping that little knife about him. He will in the future be even more so, I firmly believe.

He likes to stay at hotels like the Biltmore in New York and was doing so on a recent business trip. On his last day he scurried about the city, winding up his affairs, then returned to his room to pack quickly and make an early train. The room had been serviced, he noted, as he barged in, took off his coat and went into the bathroom, pulling the door shut. Several minutes later, he tried to open that door and nothing happened. The door knob just spun around and the latch wouldn't give and there was no budging the door. He was trapped, well and truly.

For a couple of minutes he contemplated awaiting the sometime arrival of the hotel housekeepers, perhaps the following morning. With a single window overlooking a deserted, fifteen-story airshaft, there seemed to be no other option. Then, he looked things over a little more closely, discovered a set-screw in the door knob, and went to work with his little knife.

A couple of passes and the door knob worked and the door opened and he caught his train. He is quite certain the knife saved him from a truly annoying experience.

Out of all this, what was said in the first place still holds: You nearly always have your pockets with you and one of them should have a knife in it. There are plenty of choices.

Folding Belt Knives

6 If you really wanted to, you could wear these big folding knives in your pocket. As a matter of fact, I bet over half of you do. We're going to call them folding belt knives and folders, however, to distinguish them from the generally smaller folding knives we call pocketknives.

Where might the dividing line fall? It isn't length, since there are lock-blade knives over 4 inches long that are definitely pocketknives. It isn't the locking mechanism, since there are regular springback knives that are definitely folding belt knives. I'm inclined to think weight and beef — not bulk, but sturdiness — make the difference. Let's say 5 ounces and a ⅛-inch blade stock mark the difference. We'll make an exception for 6-inch knives, too, even if they don't make the weight. Six is a lot of inches in a knife.

Knives of that weight and beef have been around in the United States a long time. There was not, however, much design choice. You could have a heavy, single saber-ground clip blade or that blade plus a long thin flat-ground skinning blade in a two-bladed

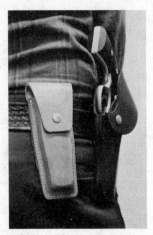

A belt folder is sometimes worn on the belt, but not always. The manufacturers seem to figure it out for you —some come with and some without holsters.

knife and you could have that identical design from all the major knife companies. And there were some oversize single-bladed jackknives. That was only a few years ago, but it is ancient history, like a turn-of-the-century Sears catalog.

Now, the world is upside down. You can shop around and fit yourself out with three dozen different heavy folders from all around the world. Even U.S. companies have given over copycatting each other and compete with new and original designs of their own. Individual knife makers have also caught the folder fire. A dozen of them are making folding belt knives at prices high enough to make a banker blanch. As a matter of fact, prices for some of the factory-produced folders would stagger your average plumber.

The Buck folder started this ball rolling some years back and remains the model for many of the knives on the market. It is a heavy knife of rosewood, brass, and steel. The blade of the original is 4½ inches long, a Bowie type combining both the saber grind and hollow grinding. It's plenty of knife for most belt-knife jobs. It probably is heavy enough to be best on a belt. Certainly, it's heavier than a great many belt knives.

The Buck is also quite handy from the sheath, even one handed. You can grasp its protruding blade between thumb and forefinger and snap the handle away from the blade. The heavy brass bolsters make this pretty easy. There is very little spring tension to work against, remember. But there is a certain amount of juggling involved and you should go slow until your fingers know what they're doing.

There are other ways to get the typical lock-blade knives open one handed. You can hold the knife across your palm, blade side away from you, and pinch the blade between your middle finger and thumb. Then wedge your fingers back against the knife's handle, which will start the blade open. When

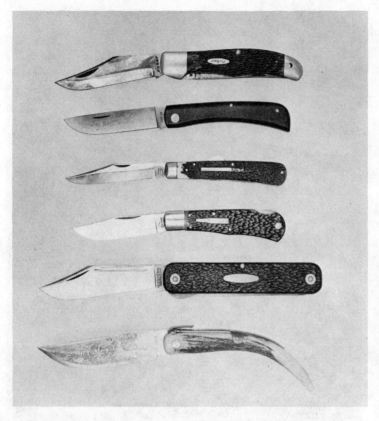

This group represents the range of belt folders — from about as small as fixed-blade knives get up to 4½ inches or so. The curved-handle model and the slim lock-blade are foreign. The other four are American.

the blade moves, press down on the blade with your thumb and keep it going. If you sweep your thumb around a half circle, the blade will follow and click open. This is another stunt to practice slowly at first, and perhaps some tape over the edge wouldn't hurt, either.

Another one-hand mode of operation involves getting the blade started and then catching the point in something solid—your belt or a piece of wood, for instance. With the point anchored, the knife snaps open easily.

I don't believe anyone could make a complete list of belt folders, but here certainly are the major brand names in the field: Buck, Puma, Case, Schrade-Walden, Kabar, Western. Besides these, which have established themselves as American brands, less

It probably isn't fair to point this out, but these four nearly identical two-bladed hunters are each by a different American factory. From the top, Case, Kabar, Schrade-Walden and Western. There was a price difference in them. The higher-priced Case and Kabar exhibit heavier swelled bolsters, more beef all around, something a little shinier in the finish department.

well-known factories in Japan, Germany, and Italy make good folding belt knives.

On the Continent, of course, they have never stopped making stout folding knives, designed for the man who takes game regularly. Many of these have been of locking design all along. Continental cutlery runs to its patterns, too. Most German folders — the typical home-consumption design — use the spear point as their basic blade. And multiple blades are more common than otherwise. A long saw is quite common, and its teeth are primarily bone rippers. A corkscrew is regarded as vital where a hunter never knows when he might run into a corked bottle.

Sometimes you'll see a Continental hunter's folder, particularly the sort that includes a vent hook—a gadget with which one draws bird intestines — with peculiar quillons. They look funny, until you figure out they are shell extractors, 16 gauge on one side and 12 gauge on the other, most likely. In the days of paper cases and gunsmith-loaded cartridges, it was most useful for double-gun shooters to have a little extra help in extracting stuck shells. One simply snapped the knife guard over the cartridge rim from the top and hauled away. Now, most of them shoot plastic cartridges, but you never can tell, can you?

The amount of work a big folding knife can do equals that of the same size fixed blade, of course. It does have a joint in the middle, which might limit its usefulness as a last-ditch lever or pry bar, and before you can use it, you have to open it. That isn't important except where the fingers are icy cold or you need the knife in a desperate hurry.

One time I saw a fellow take an elk apart with the typical Kabar folding hunter — the two-bladed non-locker—and that was pretty interesting. It was a nice, bright sunny morning and we were in no rush, so he showed us how to run the seams in the pelvis and sternum. That big saber-ground clip blade got pushed in and out, cutting first this way and then that. He pried a little—a very little—and threw his weight on one leg and then the other, and just whittled that horse-sized carcass apart. We got in more of a hurry about then, so he didn't go down the spine. In fact, he just unleashed his axe and quartered the carcass, hide and all, in about three minutes. But he convinced me — given the time, you sure can do the job with a folder.

It helps, I think, to have not only time, but good light and comfortable weather, too. Two nights earlier, with black dusk coming on fast, I had to take a deer-sized belt knife—a fixed-blade model—to an elk carcass of my own and there wasn't much finesse to

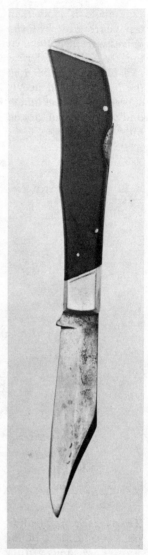

This lock-blade folder was purchased in the fall of 1917 by the father of a friend of mine and has been in reasonably steady use since, which seems to me to be fair service for less than $3. Maker? Someone in Winsted, Conn.

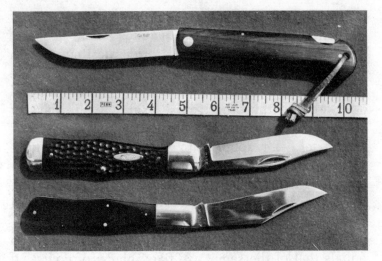

This photo is more than ten years old, but the knives were new then. At top, the Kabar bolsterless lock-blade mentioned in the text; below, a heavy, saber-ground Case hunter and a lighter, flat-ground Kabar single jack.

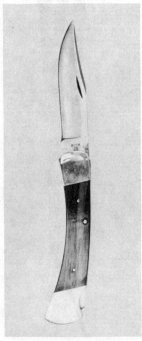

This is the pace-and-trend-setting Buck folding hunter. A heavy-duty knife, it locks open and has been found enough knife for most of the thousands of hunters who have tried it.

The heavy Buck pattern will open and lock from this position with a flick of the wrist.

that, believe me. I got a rock and drove the knife through the pelvis and then hammered it through as much rib cage as I had time for, and then I jumped on the legs to finish the pelvis job. The knife still bears the scars, but the elk ate good because I got him spread out enough to cool.

Experts do not all agree that the locking feature is needed. I like it, though.

I suppose one's attitude about the locking feature

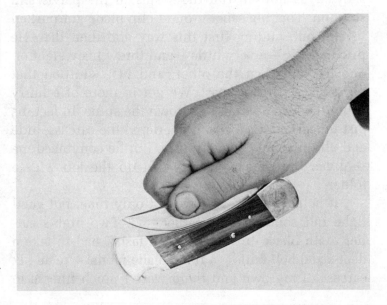

of a folding knife depends on whether or not you ever got your fingers in the way of a closing pocketknife blade. As it so happens, I have. I was quite young — not so little that anything got amputated, but I bled plenty all the way home. Modern kids don't realize how easy they get fixed. To tell you how long ago all this was, the knife involved came to me in the pocket on the side of a pair of high-tops. Sad to relate, the boots did not have copper toe caps.

Anyway, there came that little boy, white faced but not crying anymore, leaving a bloody trail down a Chicago sidewalk, and there was his mother, dealing with a deep cut in the index finger, a lesser cut in the second finger and a heavy scratch in the third finger. Band-Aids were not in the cards, not being invented yet, and a quick trip to the hospital wasn't on, since the fingers were still attached. So she did the job with gauze and adhesive tape, boiling cheesecloth for the gauze, I believe. It was quite an impressive bandage. To this day, I haven't let another knife fold back on me and I like lock-blade knives.

For five or six years, my basic pocketknife was the Case #6111½L, which is that 4¼-inch slim-

Another one-hand opening requires pinching the blade and pushing it out of its seat (left) and then continuing the push with the thumb (right). Some specimens are too tightly fitted for this when new.

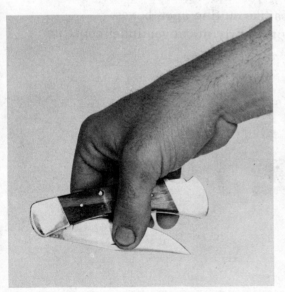
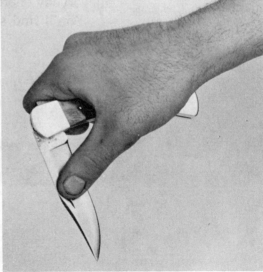

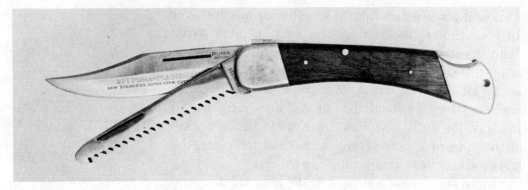

This deluxe Puma follows the Buck pattern, but provides the typical European wood-and-bone saw, making the knife extra functional at some cost in dollars and weight. Both blades lock, which makes sense.

Here is an Italian hunters' combination knife. The six blades add a small clip-cutting blade and a corkscrew to the usual four, and the peculiar "guards" are shell extractors for 16- and 20-gauge shotshells.

handled lock-blade knife — then the only lock-blade Case made — with a fairly heavy saber-ground blade and cute little dagger-style guards that popped out when you opened the blade. I wore out one of those, and finally moved on from its replacement, probably when some other lock-blade knife caught my fancy. One doesn't very often wear out a quality product, so I ought to say I was living in rural Florida during that time. Pockets full of sand are not good environments for knives. Also, I sharpened it a lot.

A lot of the big folders on the market have thin flat-ground blades in place of the wedgy saber grind most common, and that's a good thing. The heavy blade is reassuring, true, but it gets in the way of a lot of everyday chores like cutting open boxes.

You'll find some fairly unconventional construc-

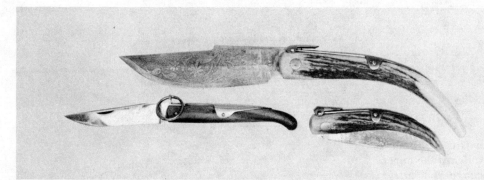

tions among large folding knives if you go looking, and some of them are pretty neat. There's almost always a good reason for the variation. For instance, there used to be, and perhaps still are, French and Spanish lock-blades, handled in horn, that don't have scales or dividers. The blade folds into a slot cut into the horn and the needed springs are pinned on the outside of the knife. The Spanish ones I have seen have a ratchet inside, and the click-clack-click when you open one of those can get you a lot of attention in a crowded room.

This pattern, with external springs and no metal in the handle, provides more blade for less weight than almost any other. You'll find knives like these in specialty cutlery stores in big cities. The matching pair are Spanish; the shiny one is French. The big one's blade is 4 inches long.

With no bolsters and no scales, there aren't many parts. The lock is on top—you pull up on a thoughtfully provided ring or lever. I have used this pattern quite a bit because it is lightweight, nice looking and handles well. All of the three I've used had good-to-excellent edge-holding capability and two of them could get sharp enough to scare you.

Kabar had a bolsterless lock-blade for a while—a big one—and I hope they still do. This was nearly 6 inches long with rosewood scales and a big stainless pin. The blade was a thin straight skinner, and worked very well in the woods. The knife was quite light for its size. It was the best solution I've seen to the weight problem any large conventional folder has.

My favorite of all large folders has become, to a degree, illegal—for what reason I know not. Up until there was a specific ruling by, I believe, the Treasury people, Garcia was importing from Finland the

71

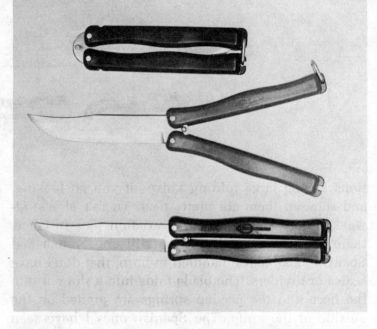

This is the Hackman Camp Knife. At the top is the package you carry; below that, the handles, swung almost through 180° to open the knife; at bottom the package you use, latched up tight again. It's the best all-around solution to the lock-blade problem, even if it does lack visual glamour.

Hackman Camp Knife. Under that name it had been and still is marketed everywhere but here. It is still on the market in Canada, I am told. The knife may not be imported, and therefore may not be sold, but it is not a sawed-off shotgun, so if you have one, keep it.

Garcia didn't kick up much fuss when told they couldn't bring it in anymore because it was never a strong seller. I don't know why what might be the best possible single solution to weight, strength, durability, and usability in a large folding knife didn't sell at $7.50, but it didn't, which shows you how much the average knife user knows.

What you got for your $7.50 was a 3 7/8 x 3/4-inch saber-ground, nicely finished straight blade with a high point that provided over 1½ inches of curved edge. The blade was made of stainless steel with genuinely superior edge-holding ability. That is, it was not only genuinely superior to most stainless-steel blades — it was generally superior, period. The knife had seven parts: the blade, three stainless-steel pins, one stainless-steel shackle-latch, and two nylon

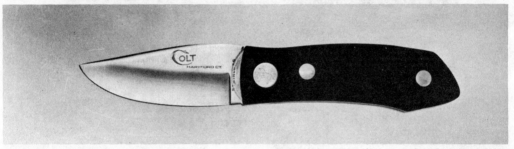

handle pieces. The design was basically Filipino, called in the Philippines a *balisong*, I believe. I have also heard it called a butterfly knife. The two parts of the handle swing around the blade on pins. At one end of their swing they surround the blade; at the other end, they come together to form a handle. It is possible to open the knife rapidly with one hand, but that is not its virtue.

The Hackman Camp Knife's principal virtue is that it is a functional design triumph. It is virtually unbreakable; it folds into a package $4\frac{3}{4}$ x $1\frac{1}{4}$ x $\frac{5}{8}$ inches when open, it is enough knife for almost any job. It rusted not and neither did it chip. The materials were cannily chosen to match the design. It weighed just 3 ounces.

It is not, admittedly, a thing of beauty. I maintain, however, that it gets prettier and prettier the longer you use it.

The nylon handles (red or black) took full advan-

Here is Barry Woods patented magic, as made for the Colt name and now discontinued. At top left, one handle side and the blade have been started spinning; at top right, the blade has stopped and the handle keeps going; below, a very solid-feeling knife is ready to use.

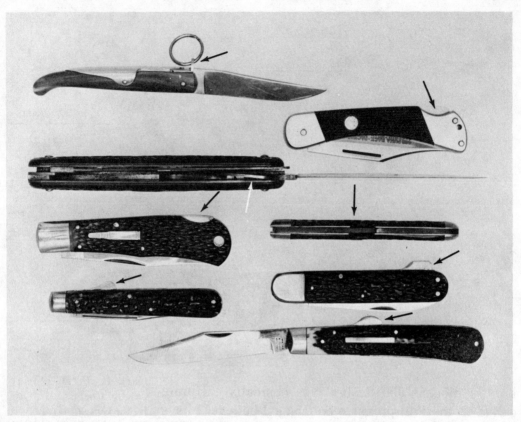

Lock-knife latches appear all over depending on the model, and range in complexity from a spring that must be pulled up (top knife), which isn't very natural, to a bent section of the handle liner (biggest knife, at arrow) which is possibly the cheapest way to lock a blade.

tage of nylon's tendency to cold-form. When the knife was latched open, and left that way a long while, the latch got a little loose. Then you latched it shut, and you got a tight latch-up because you were working against the cold-forming. And vice-versa.

I have neither seen nor heard of one breaking. When I first got my hands on one I made some noise in praise. The chum at whom this praise was leveled took it out back to "see how good it is." I got out there and found him playing mumblety-peg in a cement-block wall with it. He pried it out and handed it to me, the point undamaged. I remonstrated with him and he said, "But mine will do it," and hauled out his favorite belt folder and flang it point first into the wall. He had done it before, but this wasn't his day. Plink—off went the point.

This monster, made by Western, provides a good 4½-inch clip blade and 5-inch saw (it's their #932) making a 6-inch package not easily forgotten. The flat-ground blade is finished to thinness and cuts and slices well.

Why go on so about a cheap knife no longer on the market? Well, for one thing, I know fellows who would pay $25 or more for one, which is either a really nasty comment on the dollar or a recognition of quality. What I am really hoping is that a sensible knife-using congressman will ask the Treasury to lay off. Next best would be someone in the knife business deciding to try the design out with a "Made in America" stamp on it.

A Californian named Barry Wood invented, of all things, a new way to make a folding knife and you will run into them wearing the Colt label. No one has ever—except perhaps Mr. Wood in his patent application—successfully described in words how the knife works, but I'll try. The blade and separate sides of the handle are pinned together crossways at one end and

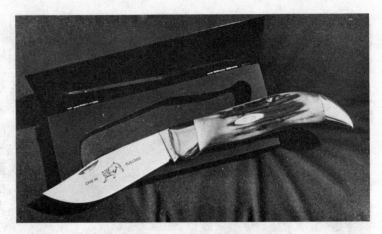

Case made this handsome Bulldog large folder starting about fifteen years ago. It's heavy and a lot of people think a knife this good should have a lock.

pivot on that pin. You lever one side of the handle up from the other side to free it, then swing it through a full circle and the blade goes with it. Half-way round, the blade stops, and when you finish the circle you have the handle in your hand and the blade ready to use. Go the other way and the swinging handle tucks the blade away again, inside the handle. It's like magic and perhaps you should look at the picture.

It is such a neat idea it will all come together some day. Colt abandoned the knife for some corporate reason or other, and the several other arrangements set up to market the design don't seem to be jelling. It has been made in some quantity in a slim version as well as the chubby Colt design, but never got to the general market.

In the main, belt folders are conventional. The latch on locking models wanders around from design to design. Some put the latch forward, but most install the lock release at the back end. One recent entry has its lock on the side of the knife. The forward releases make learning to close the knife one-handed easier, but you soon learn to make the knife swap ends so you can get at the rear latch. Don't buy one with a stiff release if you can help it. It takes a long time to ease.

A belt folder is in one respect just like a pocket-knife, as described in the last chapter. It should walk and talk, but locking models don't have that stop

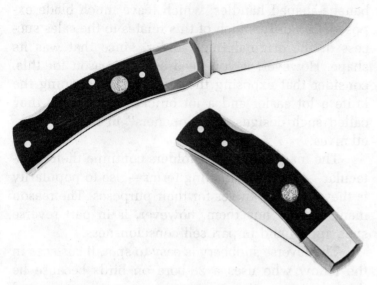

Smith & Wesson, the gun people, are now into knives and this one with a 3½-inch blade a full inch wide is not a folding knife, they say, but a hunting knife that folds.

halfway open that is characteristic of a good pocket-knife. When you get the blade almost all the way open, a correctly tuned lock-blade will snap it the rest of the way. The same thing should happen when you close the knife. The same rules of fit and finish must apply, also. Very few poor knives are finely finished.

Worrying about lock-blade belt-folder fit-up is not a waste of time. The spring tensions must be there so the closed knife stays closed until you open it. Most belt folders are quality knives and take keen edges. Without ever meeting you, I can say you do not have any desire to stick your hand into a pocket with a large, sharp, and open knife in it. It hurts and it is messy and it is time consuming because you can't always find a big Band-Aid or a small Emergency Room right away.

While we're at it, there's another drawback to the belt folder. Except for one or two special designs, it is hard to clean up. Get one full of blood and you simply won't clean it without a bucket of water. Saliva is OK, but I always feel dumb spitting into my knife, not to mention the insanitary aspect for a knife that may slice tomorrow's salami.

Latter-day belt folders show a predominance of

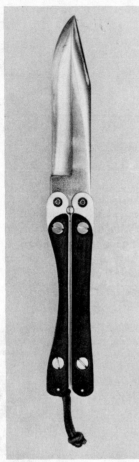

Here is a massive attempt to duplicate the Hackman Camp Knife. The heavy blade is 6 inches long, and the handle is formed of sheet stainless steel with thin wood scales. It worked, but it sure was big. This is the only one, incidentally — it's hand-made.

banana-shaped handles, which leave much blade exposed. Certainly, much of this relates to the sales success of the original Buck folder, since that was its shape. However, if you need a good reason for this, consider that exposing the blade makes opening the knife a lot easier and a lot quicker. Way back, they called such designs "easy openers" in regular pocketknives.

The main reason belt folders continue their spectacular—in knife-marketing terms—rise to popularity is they are good knives for their purposes. The reason many fellows buy them, however, is in part reverse snob appeal and in part self-consciousness.

The reverse snobbery is easy to spot. It surfaces in the fellow who uses a 28-bore on birds because he thinks it is sportier. Besides, everyone knows a real expert doesn't need a big knife. The self-conscious fellows buy them because they just can't see themselves with a sheathed knife on the belt. It probably looks good there, but this isn't the Wild West and all that. They need a stout knife, though, whether their self-image can stand it or not, so they go for the big folder. It makes sense.

There are some fellows with neither of these hangups who like the folding knives for their specific virtues: They will go in a pocket; they are very compact, either pocketed or belted; they are almost all nicely made possessions; you can have one with you almost all the time; they are safe until opened. A belted folder, by the way, is a sensible knife for the handgunner because it will live in harmony with a belted gun. Works fine either before or behind the handgun holster. With its edge and point tucked down inside, the belt folder is one useful knife you can wear out front on your belly.

The final word on belt folders is actually a question: Why not?

The Sharp Pry Bar

7 There is survival and survival. Everyone is surviving these days, it seems, and inevitably, there are survival knives. This writer collaborated in the design of one, in fact, called the Garcia Survival Knife. That knife is the logical extension of the theory of the sharpened pry bar.

The Garcia Survival Knife has (some may still be for sale) a 7-inch blade of spear-point design with saw teeth on the back. These are genuine kerf-cutting saw teeth, not mere aluminum-ripping serrations. It is possible, though very strenuous, to saw off a 2x4 with this knife. It was designed to be made by Hackman of Finland in stainless steel and the first batch were. Subsequently, the same design was fabricated in Brazil. The first thousands were awfully good knives; I have no experience with the second batch, but they are much more lightly constructed, which still leaves them heavy. (The Garcia knife was very heavy and intended to be so. I don't believe a stronger blade of ¼-inch stock was ever produced.)

I was responsible for the shape and grind of the

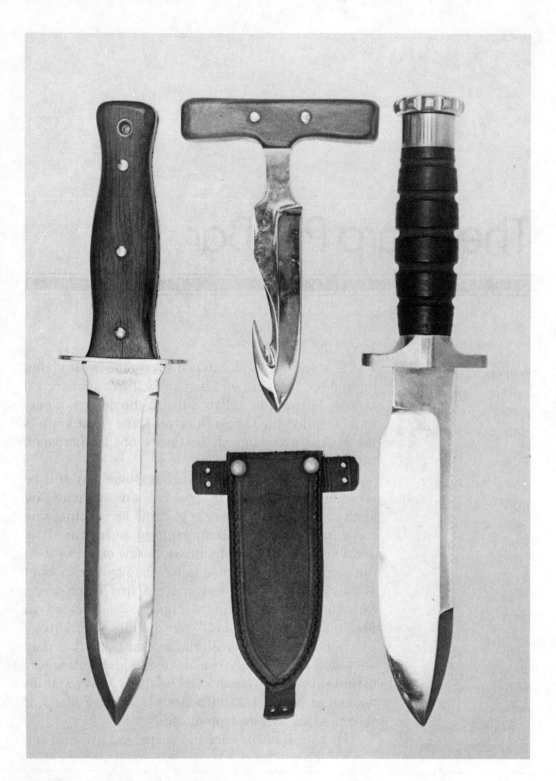

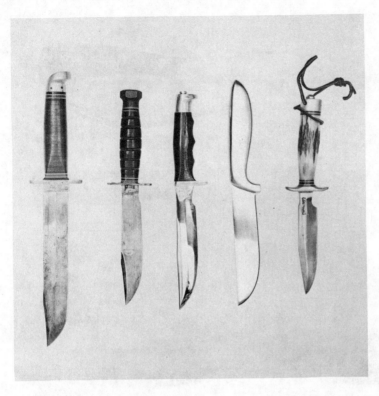

Opposite:
I designed these knives — except that Pete Dickey did the guard and handle of the knife on the right — to serve the sharp-pry-bar-survival role. On the right is the Garcia Survival, discussed in the text. The T-handled knife in the center was designed for parachutists as a panic-situation shroud cutter that could be sewn on chute pack or clothes, wherever handy or comforting. It was marketed, but didn't sell very well. The knife on the left is a single sample of a design that didn't go. The idea was to make a cheap, sturdy fighting knife to fit in the military's Kabar sheath and sell a lot of them to Marines who didn't like their Kabars. We'll never know if it would have worked, but the knife is OK, and very simple to make, and not all that bad looking.

blade and the overall configuration. My collaborator, Pete Dickey, figured out the rest of it. In essence, it has a hollow stainless-steel handle, closed watertight by a large threaded pommel. The space inside is nearly the size of two 12-gauge shotshells, which means it will hold matches, pills, another little knife, hooks and line—a whole raft of stuff that could come in handy. Pete went ahead then and designed and had packed a miniature kit that went into the sheath's pocket and had a lot of that gear in it.

(As a sidelight on that knife, Bill Moran bought 100 of them, edged them himself and sold them, furnished with his handmade sheath, to those of his customers who needed a good heavy knife and couldn't wait three years or so for one of Bill's own masterpieces. Four or five of them kicked back at him — trouble in the handle/blade joint—but that's all. I consider that good performance because almost all of

81

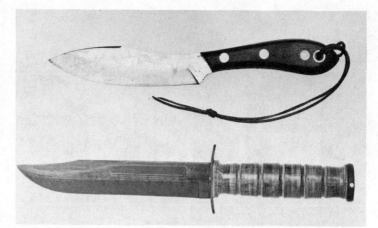

The upper knife is a big Russell Camp Knife plenty tough enough to be a pry bar; the one beneath it is the knife the Marines call the Kabar, regardless of who made it, which in this case was Camillus.

One school of pry-bar thought goes for short thick knives and here are some. The Randall at the top is actually a short 5-inch #1. Next is a knife put together with a Randall blade. The bottom knife is a very thick pry bar by Hibben.

these, by nature of the way they were sold, went to users, not collectors.)

Anyway, I put all I could think of into that knife to make it do as many jobs as possible for a fellow who, all of a sudden, has to do it all with a knife. So did Pete. It is heavy and tough enough to chop wood or meat or bone. It is wide enough to dig with if you need a hole in a hurry. The saw edge is designed to get its users poles without making loud noises. Its steel won't rust, and it's hard, so it will hold an edge. If you had to hurt someone with it, it is equal to that job. It will slice very nicely and is, after you get used to it, pretty handy for dressing out game. It has a couple of holes in the modest double guard, and by lashing through those to a pole seated in the hollow handle, a rather impressive spear results.

In all, I'm not the least bit ashamed of that knife as a sharpened pry bar.

There are quite a few heavy knives around designed for that function. They are "railroad engineered," which means they are made extra-heavy as insurance against failure. It is, after all, an imperative that a knife depended on to carry one through an emergency remain intact all the way. One is willing to make a few compromises in weight and structure to that end, even at some expense in handiness.

Other people have made other designs work, of course, and doubtless some are better. Puma has a White Hunter and a Sea Hunter which offer some very sophisticated grinding to achieve a number of blade features likely worth having. Western and Schrade and Case and Kabar all offer — or offered — heavyweight belt knives of one pattern and another.

With an eye on the jungles of Indochina, a number of firms developed combat knives, so-called, with definite heavy-duty aspects. Gerber's was a leaf-shaped double-edged dagger with a very heavy spine. Randall, always a leader, developed a range of half a dozen models. Marble's, Camillus and others mar-

Here's an "official" survival style by Randall. The ripping teeth on the blade's back are for sheet metal, not wood, and they work. This same knife is made with a tubular steel handle to put pills and stuff in.

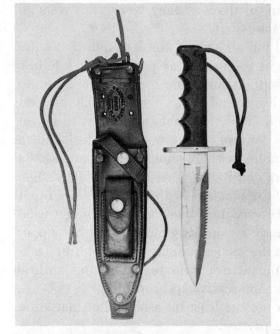

This is "el cheapo," a U.S.-issue aircrewman's knife on the Marble's pattern. It is really crude, but will work fine if it is properly manufactured. It has been made all over the world, sometimes not so well. The specimen on top, from Japan, came all unglued after a couple of days in the water. The other, by Ontario here in the U.S., is brand-new, no matter how it looks.

At the top is a current-issue knife for military parachutists. It has a pushbutton blade and a shroudcutting hook. My own T-handle knife was intended for chutists who didn't like this knife. The lower knife was the knife issued to paratroopers thirty-five years ago, so the idea must have worked out —they're still using it.

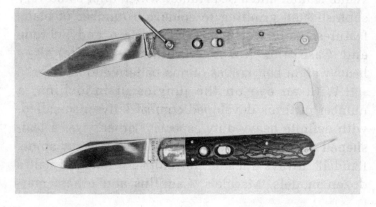

keted spin-offs and overruns of military contracts for aircrewmen's knives and the like.

In general, the blades were clipped, 5 inches or longer, with double guards and vaguely military handles — leather for many — with heavy pommels. Some had saw teeth in the back. Some were even Parkerized. Quality ranged from abysmal, for some made in Japan, to superior for, as one example, the "civilian" aircrew knives by Marble's, marketed in stores.

There are very definitely a number of aspects to survival knives, including a whole different approach entirely. But if a stout knife fits your plan, it ought to have these characteristics:

1. Five inches or more of blade, with no fragile aspects, made of 3/16-inch or thicker stock.
2. A reasonably sturdy guard on at least the cutting edge side of the handle.
3. A generous-sized handle (for maximum leverage) made of any durable material.
4. Provision for a thong or lanyard, which should be installed and left there.
5. An extra-heavy sheath, or a regular sheath reinforced. It should not be possible to fold the sheath over on itself.

If such a knife is to be prepared and then left to wait for an emergency, stainless steel is practically a must. (A knife to be carried—and cared for—often is OK in high-carbon steel.) For maximum unit strength, the tang of the blade should run the full length of the knife's handle, and full width would be preferred, theoretically.

In terms of blade design, a straight blade with a straight-clipped point is, excuse the pun, the most straightforward approach and likely to prove handiest. A saber grind — full thickness for a third of the blade width—makes a wedgy but quite strong blade. I believe some wedginess is inescapable in a heavy knife. You do not care, after all, if your salami slices

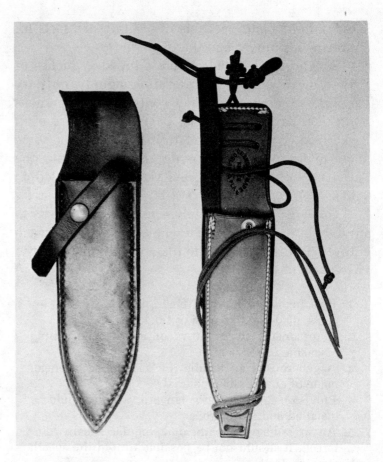

The pry-bar should be carried in something as heavy as these sheaths, which are holsters, really. Anything less solid is risky.

are a little ragged when you are happy to be slicing salami at all.

I'd like the point to be on the centerline of the knife. That is the best place for it in any thrusting blow, and it is also the place where it can be best felt while in use. Twisting leverage is not good for knife points, particularly upswept points.

The handle should be generous, and the pommel flat. Sometimes it is necessary to hammer a knife into or through something and sometimes the only hammer handy is your fist and, believe me, you don't want anything sticking up to tear up your hand. The handle material and shape should offer a good grip without too rough a texture.

Whenever the knife is put to use, even in

nonemergencies, the thong should be used. That is a very good habit that becomes absolutely essential when you face a 50-mile walk to replace the knife. For a protracted work session, the thong can be looped around the wrist; for quick cuts, a thumb through the thong laying across the back of the hand is fine. (Police officers use their batons thonged thus.) This habitual drill will, absolutely, save the knife for you some day.

The sheath should provide some reliable retainer for the knife. The thong can provide a backup system for this. Such precautions are particularly important when you're traveling on foot. The rhythm of walking can work almost anything loose, and when you're tired, you don't notice things.

In all, everything about such a serious basic tool should be first class. That doesn't mean expensive, although the heavyweights tend to cost more. It does mean that pocketbook and function should be balanced off against one another.

Why should anyone need such an item? Or, rather, who needs to do some thinking about survival knives? Well, if you do any of these things, you should have a good blade handy all the time you're doing them: off-road travel by snowmobile, horse, motorcycle, four-wheel-drive vehicle, and shank's mare; sailing, canoeing, boating *anywhere*; flying in private planes (having to remove a stout knife from my briefcase and ship it as baggage is my pet peeve about air travel); fishing almost anywhere, but particularly on streams and lonesome lake shores; long-distance ground travel by car, bus, or even train; long commutes by car; walks in forest preserves and parks with your kids; even strolls through the back forty if you live on a farm; and any sort of hunting.

A good friend of mine was headed home one evening not long ago when a nut driver bounced off another car and careened into his big Ford nearly head on. There sat Ed, very lucky, with a V-8 engine

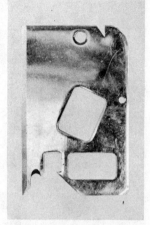

This little credit-card-sized object is a Walle-Hawk. The designer says it is the ultimate survival knife because you carry it in your wallet. It comes with a small, lengthy booklet to tell you how to use all its nifty features. I tried it and it will fit in your wallet just fine.

This is super knife, a model I don't think Bill Moran makes anymore. But if you want a knife sturdy enough for just about anything, here it is. Despite its massive design, it is quite comfortable to use.

in the passenger seat, the whole car crinkled shut, a hot smell, and gas in the air. He dug out a sturdy pocketknife in some considerable sweat, cut the jammed safety belts and kicked his way out through the windshield, using the knife to clean the jagged bits out of the frame. The car didn't catch fire, but Ed didn't know it wasn't going to when he wanted out. Without the knife, he'd have been sitting there when the fire or the police, whichever came first, arrived.

The point is that emergencies and survival situations do not permit us always to pick the time and place, and they can happen within hollering distance of the house as well as way out in the high lonesome. The unfortunate corollary is that civilization demands we leave the cold steel home most of the time. That being the case, some survival-oriented types insist that the minimum wherewithal be in their pockets all the time. And you can go a long way with a butane lighter and a small, tough pocketknife. Six feet of parachute cord and one of those trick factory-folded raincoats smaller than a pack of cigarettes are lightweight luxury. A good big handsome handkerchief (two, in fact) has lots of uses.

This isn't a book about survival, and there's a separate chapter on pocketknives, so that's enough of that, except for one last word: The careful men I know with a lot of boondock experience in the odd corners of the world carry all that stuff in their pockets, and they have a good big knife along whenever they can.

Fighting Knives

8 What is a fighting knife? In the strictest sense it is a sidearm, not a tool. The pure fighting design makes no compromise from combat efficiency. What we're talking about has been a dagger, double-edged, for most of recorded history. However, there remain a wide variety in fighting knives, based on the fighting styles planned or adopted by users. And what has become the typical American example is not double-edged. It is, of all things, a *practical* fighting knife which overlays with the emergency or survival design.

Some of the people who have used knifes as sidearms apparently planned only assassinations or fencing thrusts. Stilettos and similar designs are nothing but beefed-up ice picks. At the other extreme, some peoples and eras favored double-edged blades, wide, flat, and long. Examples are the Cinquecento Italian *cinquedea,* the Cossack *kindjal* and the Arkansas toothpick. Furthermore, all manner of short swords and special daggers have been put to combat use.

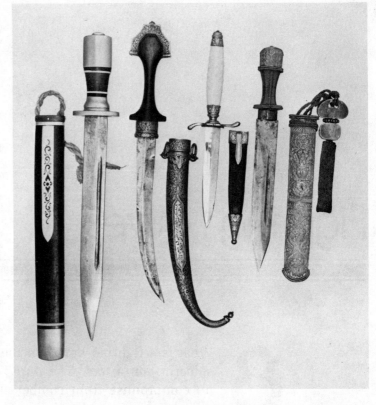

The knife is still a sidearm in societies around the world. The dagger at right center is the sort carried in South America, and not only in rural areas. The curved large knife to its left is North African, with the main cutting edge on the concave side, obviously designed for a specific style of attack. The two flankers are Tibetan, carried for all purposes by what are essentially nomads.

Given the practicalities of life, a belted knife carried *as a backup* eventually gets modified to about 6 or 7 inches of blade. Given that and the desired taper, you get a knife about 1½ inches wide at its widest. Keep this up and you get the simplest classic sort of edged weapon — a World War II Fairbairn-Sykes Commando dagger, for instance. Our Marines — some of them — were issued very similar designs in World War II.

In general, such a minimum dagger didn't make the grade with Americans. In truth, it is a dangerous knife to have around because it really will cut both ways — and often does. Beyond that, a 1½-inch-wide blade, 6 inches long, with a flat diamond cross section, slim and sharp, and designed to slip easily through clothes, skin, and meat point first, plus provide an occasional slash, breaks sometimes when an average 160-pound excited American leans on it. On rare occasions, doubtless, it's a severe case of overkill —of the knife as well.

During World War II, one fellow worked out a fighting design that caught hold and set a pattern that suited Americans then and suits them now. His name is W. D. Randall, Jr., and he signs his letters "Bo." His Randall #1 set the basic midcentury American pattern, even though he didn't make very many knives, compared to the factories. One hundred years earlier, knife-toting Americans who didn't carry a dagger type carried a Bowie pattern. Regardless of what the original Bowie was like, the bulk of the copies were 8 inches or longer, had double guards, and broad blades with clip points. They were not auxiliary weapons in the time of single-shot pistols—they were part of the main show. Laws were even passed against them.

Then came Colonel Colt and his reliable repeating revolver. The belt knife became an auxiliary, and the Bowie shrank. From 1870 or so on the pattern remained, but an 8-inch blade now marked a big knife; the bulk of them were 6 inches or less in the blade. They were still broad and had clipped points, though the double guard began to disappear.

From then on, an American pattern was set. The melting pot drew many other designs and variations, of course. In a hundred years, Americans will try almost anything, perhaps especially knives. Clip points and the broad — or medium-wide, anyway — blades remained, centered in the mainstream.

When Bo Randall set out, in genuine patriotism, to furnish American fighting men with the best fighting knife he could, he made a soldier's knife, not a blade for an assassin or a swordsman. He made those too, but his #1 is true blue, star-spangled, all wool, and a full yard wide. And it works.

The blade is 7 or 8 inches long, forged of ¼-inch high-carbon steel, straight and wide enough to provide an edge with some sweep (curve) in it. The point

This trench-knife design was thought quite the military stuff in World War I and was still issued as World War II opened. It's now considered an awkward beast, hard to carry and difficult to use. This particular specimen is, incidentally, a fake actually made in the 1960s.

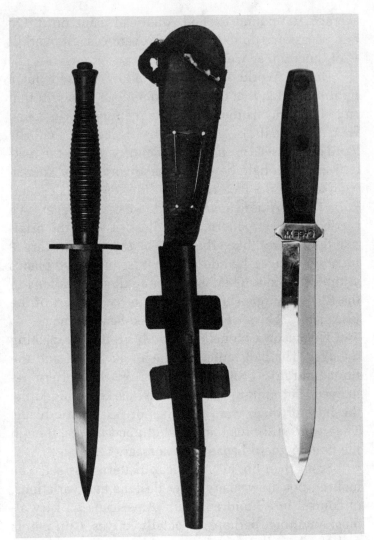

Here are two knives designed for the attack, for — to be entirely factual — killing. That on the left, with sheath, is a British issue dagger, the Fairbairn-Sykes fighting knife. It is lethal and it is handsome, but our troops found it fragile and not very useful for chores. The knife at right is designed for the same job. It is a Case XX butcher's sticking knife of old pattern, slim, tough, and very sharp. It probably isn't made anymore.

is in the center, and there is a fairly long straight clip. The false edge is sharpened — that is peculiar language, I know, but it is precise because any extra edge on a single-edged blade is called the false edge, even if it is genuinely sharp. There is a pronounced ricasso (the square section between the cutting blade and the guard). The edge of a Randall #1 is nearly in line with the user's knuckles.

Given those parameters, the grind pattern of the Randall can hardly be improved for strength reten-

Bo Randall made the double-edged dagger and kept it stout (top), but his best design is the new classic in fighting knives, the Randall #1, also shown. It fights as well or better than the double-edge and works its way doing chores as well.

tion. The stock remains full thickness along the spine, and for nearly half the width and very nearly to the point. The result is a pretty sophisticated sharpened pry bar. It is in fact and theory somewhat wedgy, but in practice it gets by fine in slicing chores because the wedge is quite long. A Randall #1 is far from an ideal hunter's knife, but it will serve.

The double guards of the #1 are relatively small, gracefully shaped, and made of nickel-silver or brass. Handle materials vary greatly, from ivory to leather; the construction varies also, with some knives handled with simple blind tangs and most with full-length narrow tangs, secured by a nut in the pommel. I have never seen a Randall #1 with insufficient handle.

Put an early World War II #1 beside Korean era #1 and you will see the design refined. The early ones weren't nearly so pretty, though all the design features were there. Whether he likes it or not, nearly every knife designer since has started from — and finished close to—the refined Bowie by Randall. That goes for factories as well as individual craftsmen.

For all the stoutness and size, the Randall #1 retains the essential features of the knife as weapon. These include a centered point for the thrust, the double edge for penetration, the doubled guards to protect and secure the hand during violent action, and

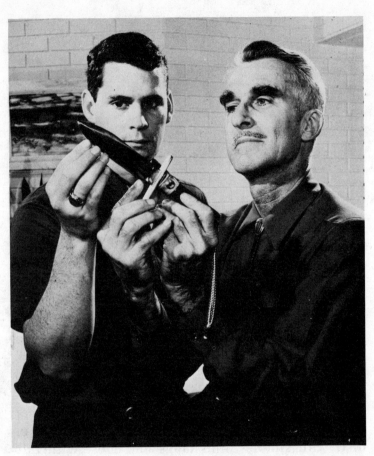

the balance toward the rear so the point may be maneuvered easily.

About knife fighting itself, this writer has little to say. Bloody men rarely write and writing men don't often get bloody—at least not from choice. Secondhand, then, I can tell you that if you have ever attended an amateur fencing meet—a local one with no champions around—you have seen knife fighting in its essentials. The participants are highly nervous; when they get wound up tight enough, they go, regardless; the winner is usually the attacker. There is none of the grace and class of cinema swordsmanship. They stumble going in; they try unconventional or panic strokes and sometimes make one good; they dominate or are dominated as much by lethal intent as

These three knives were attempts to solve the fighting man's knife problem and retained, you can see, the Randall solution. The center knife was made by Draper; the others are Hibbens. The big one with a hint of Gurkha kukri in its profile was remarkably unsuccessful, its owner told me. Draper and Hibben are inactive knife makers at this writing.

physical ability. And it is usually over in one passage. When the attacker misses or is, to coin a phrase, foiled, the attacked nails him.

By and large, Americans have been fighting physically smaller peoples for nearly two generations. The knife-attack style that works takes full advantage of the good-big-man axiom: Go in fast and hard and knock him over if you don't get the knife in. So I am told by men who have been there. Those same men tell me it could be different against a 6-foot 180-pound opponent. Then—it's the amateur fencing match all over again, and trained muscles make a difference, all else being equal, and any sane man would try to avoid having all else equal.

There is a great vogue these days for what is called a boot knife. A boot knife, in the usual meaning, is a fighting knife designed for concealment, a sort of edged snubbie. The design concessions take several forms, but inevitably involve smaller size, lighter construction, lighter weight. Handles are shorter and some, in fact, are intended to butt into the palm of the hand. Guards are either diminutive or eliminated. Flatness is a virtue in a boot knife and there are designs with one-sided grips. All that still adds up to a

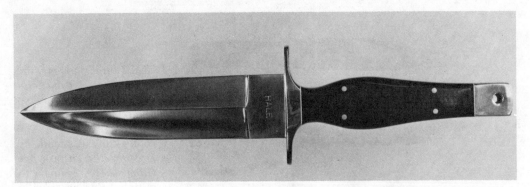

A broad double-edged dagger, like this by a knife maker named Hale, is less specialized than the slim pattern, but in my opinion not as useful for general purposes as the more typical single-edge-plus-false-edge style.

Randall's response to later wars was the brutalizing of his #1 into beefier pieces that retained some of the fighting features, but would also open steel drums, split helicopter sides, and chop wood. This, his #14, is called the "Attack-Survival."

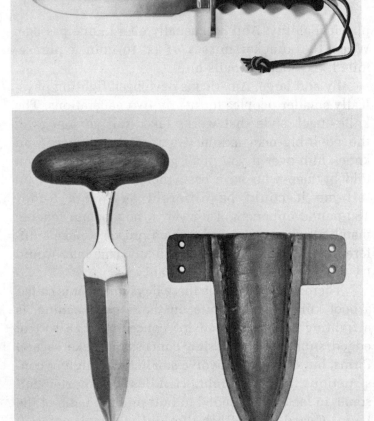

This strange beast is a push dagger, and its sole virtue is that it is very short overall. The only blow it strikes is a punch, however, and the layout permits cutting strokes only to the practiced.

96

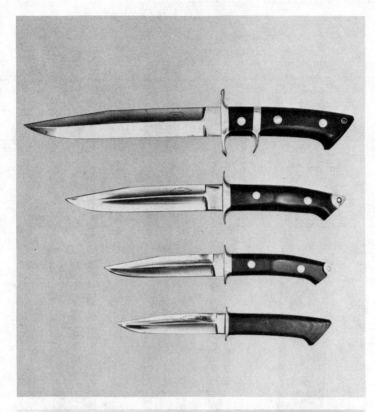

This quartet by the great Bob Loveless shows, I believe, the highest possible degrees of refinement and sophistication — not even counting mere decoration — of the basic Randall layout for a fighting knife. Loveless's names for these are, from the top, the Big Bear, the Fighting Knife, the Boot Knife and the Mini-Boot Knife. They are deeply double-hollow ground, with full tapered tangs, and elegant lines, and result in most unusually lively knives. The extra hilt on the Big Bear is called a subhilt and its purpose is to provide a firm anchor from which the index finger can position the point as well as a place to haul on if the knife gets stuck.

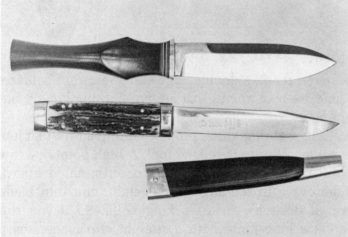

Here is a pair of boot knives. At top is the current Morseth design. The other is the current Puma. Neither is cheap; both are nicely made minimum knives for concealment.

The armies of the world seem to have decided their soldiers' need for a large knife is real, and began in World War II to furnish bayonets adaptable to knife use. The U.S. bayonet-knife (at right) of World War II was sufficiently successful that U.S. bayonets since share its features (while, at the same time, real knives were also furnished some groups). The bayonet at left is the current Finnish issue, and is the only bayonet I've seen I wouldn't mind gutting a deer with. The sheath is the issue model, too. With rare judgment, you can see, the Finns give their soldiers puuko bayonets carried as the puuko is carried.

centered point, a double edge and a rearward balance. There are boot knives that are not fighting knives, but not many.

The fighting knife, properly designed for that job, is not an all-purpose edged tool. A high point or a low point, weight forward, single or eliminated guard, more curve in the edge, less weight, and thin blade are all desirable in a working knife. So if you run across a long knife with a straight clip blade, sharp false edge, thick spine, and double guards, and it sits up in your hand looking for a place to poke, it's a fighting knife.

Specialized Knives

When you really get involved with knives, you learn that no one knife can do everything conveniently. The rule remains that any steel cutting edge is better than none, but for some jobs, some knives are immeasurably better than others. For people who work with knives extensively, the subject gets very complicated.

I once spent an enthralled evening listening to a former Maryknoll missionary describe the knives of the people he had tended far up the Amazon. They had set up a Brazil-nut industry with a processing and packaging plant, but all the outside work was done with knives. As he put his pants on each day, each man picked up his basic knife, a 14-16-inch light machete, by choice a Collins. With that he did all his personal chores; no matter where he went or what he was doing, he always had that knife with him.

Then, for ordinary work—cutting back the plants around a garden plot, traveling any trail left unchopped for three days, cutting a little grass for fodder—he used a similar machete something over 20 inches long. Again, this is a relatively light blade, and again, the common Collins pattern was the most popular.

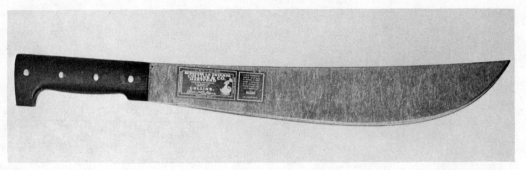

This is the top dog in bush knives —the noted Collins machete, none genuine without the mark. Different shapes and sizes abound, but this is the classic and most generally useful shape in lengths to two feet.

When there was a great deal of grass-cutting or light bush to clear, a heavier, even longer machete came into play. This was a work knife, pure and simple, 26 inches or longer in the blade and somewhat wider than the others. It retained a point, but it was too big for ordinary chores.

Finally, for the heavy work of the Brazil-nut gathering, there was a big chopper. This knife was 2 feet or so in the blade, twice as wide as the others, and had a rounded tip. With this, they could take down trees, chop open very hard nut cases, or clean out a fresh trail on a compass heading.

Smaller knives? Not many and not much need, the missionary said. "They were awfully competent with those small machetes" was the way he put it.

A good machete is a useful knife in a lot of places outside the jungle as well as in. Its chief charm is that it packs a lot of cutting into relatively little weight. A machete isn't in the same league with an axe if you're chopping trees, but then an axe isn't much good cutting grass.

The Collins, with its rectangular black paper guarantee on the blade, is the standard article of trade, though it is now made in Guatemala instead of Connecticut. Tons of similar long knives are made in Spain and Germany every year, but the consumers— the jungle people and the peons of South America— buy the Collinses first and only then the others. The knives come in a bewildering variety of pattern, ex-

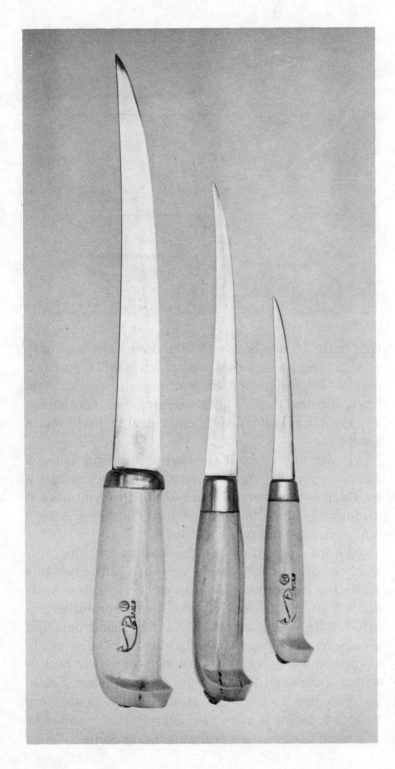

These — and others just
like them — are the main
attraction in fish knives.
All are Martiniis's sold as
Rapalas. I use the biggest
—about an 8-incher —for
a lot of meat carving, too.

These are a partial selection of various shorter working-butcher tools. The names change, sometimes, but if you call these, from the top, sticker, butcher, sheep skinner, boning, and ripper, most old-time meatcutters will know what you mean. Any of them could be adapted to meet an outdoorsman's needs. These particular ones are made by the John Russell Cutlery Co.

cept in the United States: Of late, there have been only 14-, 18-, and 24-inch patterns, which is still a gracious plenty. They also remain pretty cheap, the shortest being still less than $5 at this writing. For that money, you get a thin knife of very tough steel that will take a good edge.

If you don't take it slow while learning to use a machete, you can sprain a wrist. It's important that it be sharp — file sharp will do — and that you drag it through the cut, slicing rather than chopping. After a while, you get pretty good at it.

There are other jungle knives besides the machete, of course. Most are very heavy. The two this writer has had experience with are a Senegalese knife and a British-issue jungle knife. Both were military in origin. The Senegalese knife was both handsome and a fearsome weapon. It had a hardwood handle, nicely shaped, and a heavy blade—¼ inch or more at back— with a square end. It came with a good leather sheath, but you had to have the strength of a Senegalese trooper to swing it more than a dozen times, and even so it didn't cut any better than a lighter knife.

The British knife looked like an oversize butcher knife, about 16 inches long and 3 inches wide, and had its weight toward the tip. The grip was made of two flat pieces of brown plastic, riveted on with copper rivets. It was a pretty good knife. On one occasion I used it to chop down two or three 8-inch softwood trees and then render them into short logs for a corduroy path to an Everglades outhouse. It worked fine, but a longer knife made more sense and I no longer own it.

I have also tried all sorts of U.S.-marked bolos. Of these, all I can say is that soldiers must have been more muscular in those days. They were all lousy bush knives.

Owning a machete for once-in-a-while excursions may be difficult to justify, but how about making one a part of your garden tool set? The neighbors may blink at first, but sooner or later, they'll all try to borrow it. There is no better tool for trimming pruned or fallen tree limbs into bundle length, selectively cutting weeds, or beating multiflora rose hedges back where they belong. For that work, get the big one. The little short one is for lashing to the packframe, as here it rides lighter than a hatchet.

A sheath is a problem. The only solution is to make your own, for a properly sharp machete is certainly not safe in the flimsy canvas pouches you find in surplus stores. Why don't they all have sheaths? Well, a good sheath would cost more than the knife, but, more than any other reason, the machete is a knife carried in the hand.

There are other work knives to be considered.

Fish knives are pretty important to the business of making usable food out of scaly bodies. For really big fish you're going to cook whole, a slim stiff knife to rip them open is all it takes. Things get a little more complicated if you want to filet your fish.

There are apparently two schools of thought on filet knives—flexible and rigid. The flexible knife gets my vote, because it gets the most meat for the least effort. You simply start the blade where the meat is thickest at the backbone and flex it while cutting to slide close to the ribs. The thicker fish knives waste a little meat in the hollow places. On the other hand, they last longer, and perhaps hold a working edge a little longer. Ordinarily, a filet knife disappears into its sharpening stone. However, breakage is also a factor. They are thin and they are flexed and sometimes they're used for jobs they're not designed to do. It's pretty easy to break one.

I don't think anyone makes better filet knives than Martinii of Finland. Their knives are marketed here under the Rapala brand name, although nearly any Finnish knife you pick up is likely to be a Martinii, particularly plain knives. There are four sizes that I know of. The smallest has a 5-inch blade; the largest is 15 inches or so. They come with pretty good leather sheaths, the biggest one costing $10 or so in a discount house.

Fish knives should be stainless steel—most are— for the nature of their trade promotes oxidation.

On the theory that thin knives cut better, I have from time to time carried a sheathed filet knife as a basic belt knife. It works. However, you have to carry something else for prying cuts and heavy work. I think a fellow who habitually carries a hatchet in the woods could do worse than carry a large Martinii filet knife at his belt. Kept sharp, it surely turns game animals into meat at a great rate.

For some people the thicker saber-ground fish and filet knives are good basic belt gear. If a fellow likes a long, straight edge, and many do around camp, a fish knife is a pretty inexpensive answer. For some reason, the same length of edge in a "hunting knife" pattern is priced higher.

Butcher's implements, all designed before the freezer and the bandsaw took most of the poetry out of butchering, are useful possibilities as work knives.

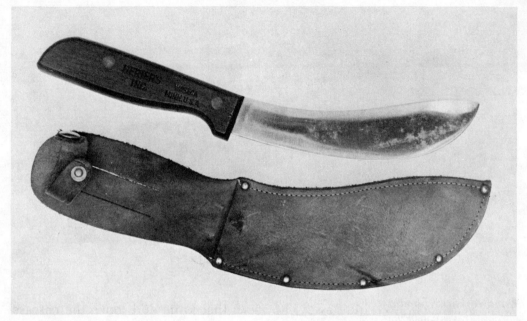

Professional meat-cutting gear is not usually hardened to the degree sporting knives boast, but that makes them easy to sharpen, which is the idea. Certainly it is difficult to imagine anything better for managing game carcasses than what professionals use on sheep, hogs, and beef carcasses.

The biggest problem with this theory is that the professionals work with a rack of knives nearby and a sharpening steel at their belt. They make a half-dozen cuts; then take a few passes with the steel; then a few more cuts; and a few more sharpening strokes. They sharpen their knives unconsciously, as part of the rhythm of their work.

I've watched a good man in a country slaughterhouse. Once the beef is killed and hoisted by its heels, he makes a bleeding cut, often with a two-edged sticking knife. Then he racks that knife and takes a short ripper and runs up the belly line and the legs. He racks that, picks up a curved skinning blade, and starts peeling off the hide, dropping it, the head and the hooves on the floor. As a helper drags the

Here's the real skinning shape, useful on large animals' hides, and also, if you take the time to learn it, pretty handy in a kitchen. Herter's gets theirs up with a sheath, which is useful for stowing the knife in a pack.

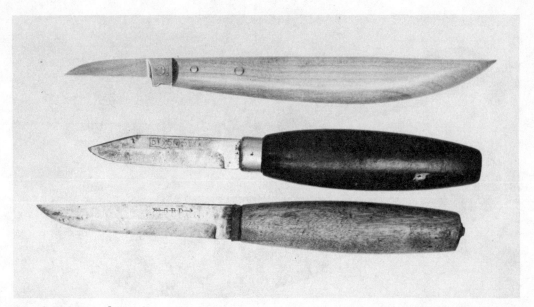

Woodworkers' general-purpose knives can be various shapes. The top one is a Brookstone Special, and is about as handsome as a useful artifact gets. The center one is a common American Dixon, sold everywhere. The bottom knife is a similarly common Scandinavian pattern, but is distinctive for me because it belonged to the cabinet-making Norwegian grandfather whom I never met.

hide away, he racks that knife and looks the carcass over, spraying and wiping any smudges—which are few—and then cleaning the floor. The ripper comes out again and he makes a gut pile, sawing through the ribs. After the "liver and lights" are retrieved, the guts are hauled out and he takes a boning knife and trims up inside. Then an electric saw cuts the carcass into two sides down the backbone. The whole operation takes about ten minutes and he uses about six knives. It takes another three or four, maybe more, knives to do a classic job of butchering the sides into useful meat cuts.

It's a little difficult to pick one tool out of that whole process and make do with it, but that's what's demanded here. It can be done, however. After all, our mountain men went "up to Green River" with similar blades. ("Up to Green River" is jargon meaning a job's well done. The words "Green River" appear several inches behind the point of the mountain men's favorite brand of butcher knife.)

There have been, past and present, what we might call patent knives. The current model is called the Wyoming knife. It consists of two finger holes, a finger rest, and two short blades that stick out in opposite directions. I have played with one and looked at it closely, but I never used one. There is a movie of the Wyoming knife at work and it looks like a whizbang. The fellow who knows how can sure zip open an animal with it, according to the movie. It's a very compact design, and once you got very good with it, you could probably use it to good effect as a somewhat awkward knife; but in the main, it is not a knife, not in the terms of this book. It is a highly specialized tool. And I for one am never going to fool with it. I'm not sure I'm smart enough.

A friend of a friend takes to the woods with a Stanley utility knife and a box of fresh blades. The Stanley utility knife is that cast metal handle held together with coin-slotted screws that uses razor-blade type replaceable blades. My friend's pal likes a sureenough sharp edge and he doesn't want to fool around sharpening it so he has learned how to get his jobs done with this knife which offers, at full extension, about an inch and a half of sharp, straight edge and a very fine point. This is another one I'm not going to fool with, but it probably works.

You'll see a fellow in the woods once in a while with a linoleum knife and he makes a hawkbill blade look like a good idea. I once ran across a surgeon doing up a deer with scalpels, and I wouldn't be surprised some day to see an X-Acto knife put to use on a deer.

There are special knives related to all manner of trades and avocations. They'll all work, but they're not the blades of choice without prior experience.

This is sold as a special woodworker's knife by Brookstone. The old-time blacksmiths called them farrier's knives. Similar patterns, made and used in pairs —one lefthanded and one righthanded — were used in the north to make snowshoes, canoes, and other needed instruments. Sometimes they were called "crooked knives" which means there are two kinds of crooked knives, because in some places they call the big skinner crooked.

107

Knives For Wives

10 I don't believe a good set of cutting edges will save a marriage, but it sure will cut down frustration in the kitchen. For twenty dollars and ten minutes every two weeks, things can be really sharp out there around the sink.

You do have to gauge your wife. Mine prefers stainless knives, not for their edges, not for their looks, not for their shapes, but simply because they don't discolor. The carbon-steel knives she uses aggravate her, because she feels she must steel-wool them to get them clean, and because if she doesn't dry them off, they'll rust. She's wrong about cleaning them, but she's right about the rust.

So there are always a couple of stainless-steel belt knives out there, proving that good all-around design is adaptable. As this is written, the favorites are a Russell Boat Knife in stainless, and a Hackman Camp Knife. They do the bulk of the work, even though their wedgy—for work knives—blades seem to me to get in the way. How I look at it is this: When Mrs. Warner gets to the woods, she'll already know how to use a belt knife.

There are about $15 worth of plain knives to back those up. A 6-inch Case Old Forge butcher knife; an Olsen Coho filet knife; a Case paring knife; a Herter's heavy curved slicer with 7-inch blade. These have been skinning knives—the big, thin crooked knife—in kitchens in the past, and very useful they are in preparing vegetables.

With not much effort, such knives are kept sharp, and with a choice of several all the time, the lady has a sharp cutter for every job. Visitors get a little envious, frankly.

Any good hardware store should have these plain carbon-steel working knives in stock. They are very like professional butcher tools, but not quite. The butcher doesn't get so nice a handle, but he gets a polished blade. In the kitchen grade, the butcher knife gets a sharper clip and a finer point than in the professional model. The really big slicers and scimitars aren't offered, but then the professionals don't get much in the way of paring knives and the like. Skinning knives don't show up in the kitchen grade, either. Some hardware stores, of course, carry the professional stuff also.

There is not much to choose between the steels of the professional and the household knives. I have had quite a happy relationship with these edges. In fact, eight, at least, of ten have proven up to quite high standards, surpassing some belt knives in this regard. I never tried to make one "sharp enough to shave," but they have certainly been consistently sharp enough to work.

A word about kitchen cutting surfaces is in order here. There is a pernicious and unfortunately successful campaign afoot to sell plastic cutting boards to housewives. They have great sanitary and upkeep advantages since they may be washed in the dishwasher. However, they are tough on the sharp edge. Since this device has gone into use in my own kitchen, the edges of all the knives dull faster, particu-

This is our family knife rack, total investment, not counting the knife at left, under $20. These knives give good service and six can be duplicated in almost any hardware store. The first knife is a Russell Boot Knife in stainless steel and costs fairly heavy money. Next is a Herter's, bought out of the catalog, then there are three Case XX knives, an Olsen Coho filet knife and an ordinary serrated bread knife. A stiff 6-inch boning knife could be added and, sooner or later, a 12-inch slicer — these aren't needed, but they'd be nice. The magnetic rack shown is a very good idea. Don't keep really sharp knives in a drawer because they cut people.

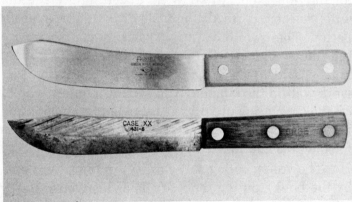

The quality of these two knives is comparable, although the finish is different. The upper knife is built for the butcher trade. It is polished to wipe easier and practically pointless because the butcher picks up a knife with a point when he needs one. The other is a hardware-store purchase now on duty in its seventh year. The sharp point is sometimes useful and the forging marks left in the blade are no problem since knives aren't in constant use in the home. A fellow could make up a sheath and carry this one in the woods and find it no liability at all.

111

The upper knife here has been around the kitchen a year or so and gotten right popular. When the smaller one, which is actually a Russell Boat model and came with a sheath, arrived and got put to use in a hurry, I wondered why. Only now have I realized that it's because it is so very like the big one.

larly at the spot where the straight runs into the curve, this being the place that hits the board and stays in contact with it. Wood is the right surface for cutting, plain wood without resin binder in it, I might add.

Having a plain carbon-steel knife is the only way for the non-expert to know he is getting a blade that will sharpen correctly and stay sharp for a useful period. There are other approaches, of course, involving more money. Gerber's original line of shiny knives, sold in jewelry and gift shops in the old days, work well in the kitchen. And I know a fellow who bit on the Cutco line of knives sold by appointment only, like Fuller brushes. In fact, I was invited to the house for the presentation.

The young collegiate salesman produced his spiel by the book, touting the marvels of his wares. He cut slices of bread in half, which doesn't sound like much of a stunt except he did it in such fashion he got two full-size thin slices. He performed feats of magic with tomatoes and the like, ribboned up cabbage, and all of that, but these all paled into insignificance alongside his best stunt. He had one of us hold a length of 1½-inch Manila line out between our hands and,

112

with one slash of a kitchen knife, cut it in two. It was marvelous.

My friend bit for $100 worth of knives and five years later still swears by them. All have serrated edges; all are good-looking; all are good kitchen knives. I tried to set aside enough time to figure out why, but have not yet done so. My friend says they're not really knives, but very specialized chisels and the edge seems to support this thesis.

There are other much-vaunted kitchen knives around. Some like to fool with Oriental cookery and use those knives, but I have not. There are widely advertised sets of French chefs' knives and I have tried those. Some have been technically very good, but the shapes don't suit me and would require my hands to relearn all the chores.

Presumably, the same people — Case, Schrade, Olsen et al.—who make good plain knives make good fancier knives. I haven't tried them. I would say that only high-priced stainless knives would be as good as the regular carbon-steel knives. Unfortunately, there don't seem to be many non-stainless sets of matching kitchen knives around.

With all these various knives available, which ones does your kitchen need? There should be two paring knives and whether or not they are identical doesn't matter. What does matter is that two will stay sharp twice as long as one. Next, get a boning knife—

This close-up of the Cutco knife edge tells you why it is so efficient. The edge is made up of a number of chisels spaced between cutting points—all angles, no curves. But when the points go, and this knife is about five years old, the edge has to go to the factory to get sharp again. It gives good kitchen service, though: You just set the blade on the work and push straight down.

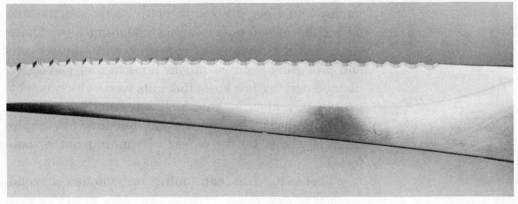

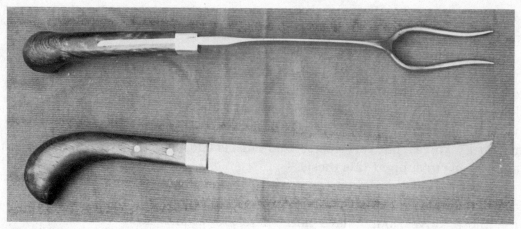

a 5-incher will do. Then the 6-inch butcher-bladed knife is a necessity. The only other requirement is for a long blade—8 inches or more. In my house this is a filet knife, but they are hard to sharpen because the blade is so flexible. A longer butcher knife—9 inches, perhaps—would make sense, but if you could find a good ham slicer, particularly a plain professional slicer like the fellow uses in the cafeteria to slice your sandwich beef from the full round, you'd be well served.

Even in these inflated times, a $20 bill is important money in this class of merchandise. But for grand occasions, when you will be carving in the presence of all, a special carving set is justified. The Gerber's are very, very good. If you have your grandfather's old set, it's probably pretty good, too. It is worth the money and time it takes to get a really sharp outfit consisting of a long knife and matching fork. These are a lifetime investment requiring only annual care and providing peculiar satisfactions in use. The secret of good carving is a knife that cuts well, which is why people buy electric knives. (I have nothing against electric knives. They do the job, but they're complicated. Perhaps I have a fear of running out of batteries.)

That's it. You can outfit the kitchen beyond

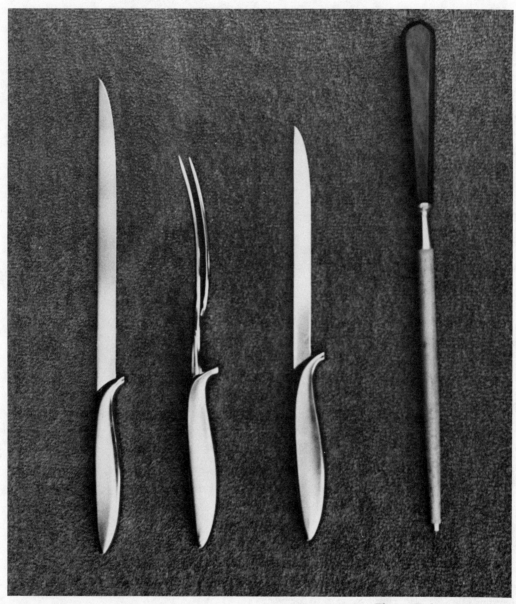

legitimate complaint for about $20 or you can go to $150. Either way, you stand to gain. When a kitchen operator first lays hands on good cutlery, a great light dawns. Knives are crucial in a kitchen.

These Gerbers give good service on dressy carving occasions. I've not found very many of the similar-looking sets on the market as good as those with the marking, "Gerber Legendary Blades." These are nice tools.

Buying Your Knife

11 The cutlery business, as much as any labor-intensive undertaking, depends on the hands of men. Cutlers are skilled laborers, highly skilled laborers.

Certain sorts of knives are truly machine made, and certain good knives—such as those with cast-in-place handles—are largely machine made, but most knives are mostly handmade. The difference between the one-at-a-time knife and the mass-produced article is largely that the factory product is turned out by many pairs of hands. There is no basic reason why the end result of mass production should not be superiority. Indeed, some factories achieve it regularly.

Very cheap knives of complicated pattern—blade, handle, fittings and sheath that look like more expensive models — are likely to be unsatisfactory. Even cheaper knives of less pretension with, for example, plain wood handles riveted on, no high polish anywhere, and no sheath furnished, can be very good indeed. It's in part a question of where the maker spends the money.

Almost any knife is made of some type of steel. If

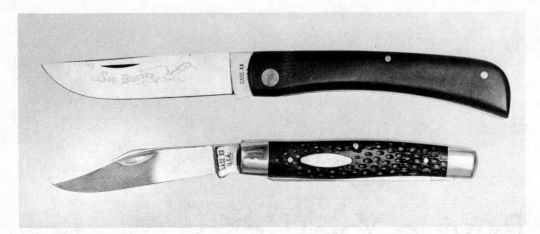

The finish of any knife is part of its price. The lower knife is finished to a high degree of polish all over and is predictably high priced. The upper knife is what might be called plain finished. It is smooth, of course, but the blade surface is relatively dull. In this example, the upper knife is considerably simplified, too. Such differences are not rip-offs, but rather a serious attempt to continue to give good value at something remotely resembling the good old prices. Sometimes, you get what you didn't pay for, but most times you get what you did.

the particular sample at hand got the right heat-treatment, it could be almost as good as a knife can be, by accident as it were, no matter how cheap. The writer remembers how he learned this very well. The knife in question was the plainest sort of pocketknife, costing 89¢. (The same knife is now $3.89.) Its handle was a piece of steel folded to shape and painted black; its blade was a plain spear point. That knife would take a shaving edge and hold it.

Well, I marveled at it, and bought a couple more and put them in a drawer. When a friend admired a little job of cutting for the second time, I took the hint and gave him the knife. The punchline you know: Neither of the other identical knives I had matched the first, nor did four or five more I tried. They were worth 89¢, but that was all.

Accidental quality is not, of course, what any consumer seeks. Nevertheless, just as a percentage of the total production of any knife will have softer steel than the rest, so will a percentage of the total be superior.

As we have mentioned, high-carbon steel is worked soft, then heated red hot and quenched, then reheated (tempered) to working strength. In the mechanics of mass production, the great majority of blades will get the average treatment and are tem-

pered to an average. A few blades will get too soft and probably not pass inspection; a few are equally bound to wind up at the high end of the specifications.

There is, unfortunately, no way to tell one from the other. I had an old-timer friend once who wouldn't buy a knife that wasn't extra-sharp as it came from the factory, but I'm afraid some good sharpeners on the production line beat him from time to time. At any rate, I didn't think his knives were anything special. They weren't bad, either — it takes pretty fair steel to get good and sharp, so maybe his wasn't such a bad approach. He just got a bunch of knives out on the counter and tried them on his thumb until one suited him.

The best guarantee of quality is a good name and, unfortunately, a fair price. It's also a good idea to buy a knife from a retailer who can afford to pay some attention to you if you have a beef. Big-discount operations can't. It is just not in their nature. To expect a low, low price and courtesy and unfailing attention to a low-mark-up sale is an elegant dream, and that's all. But the local guy who gets his price and wants your business will listen.

If you can't find what you want—or simply want a bigger than local selection—you have to go where they are, of course. Sometimes that means buying on out-of-town trips, and sometimes that means mail-order from special outfits advertising in firearms and

Another factory move to upgrading is the high-finish special model, like this Kodiak by Case. You pay a premium, and you get a fancy knife.

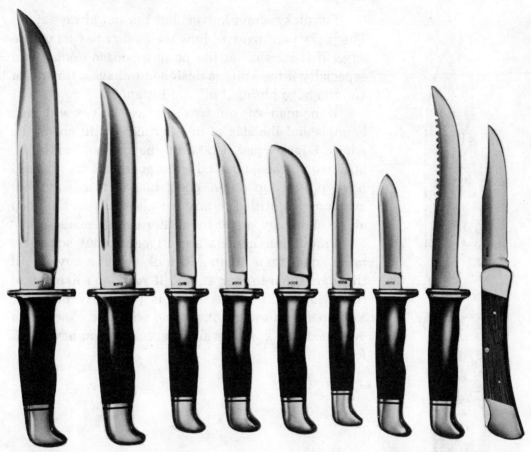

sporting publications. Indeed, it might mean the giants like Sears and Montgomery Ward.

The best way is to see and handle the specific knife in a retail store. Ruskin's advice is solid stuff: If you pay high and get what you want, you just lose the extra money; if you pay low and don't get what you want, you have lost the whole price.

However, old names in mail-order merchandising don't get old cheating people. Quite the contrary is true. I have dealt for years with one fairly posh mail-order outfit and have never been disappointed. Another distinctly non-posh, but very big, sporting-goods mail-order shop always delivered good value. I didn't always like the stuff, but I never had a legitimate beef.

Shapes and sizes can be pretty confusing. These nine knives by Buck by no means cover all the possibilities. There is no substitute for handling the knife you think you want, even if one of these shapes looks like just the thing to you.

121

I'm picky about knives, but I'm not always right. The picky part involves how the factory has set up the edge. If it runs off at the point or doesn't edge, and especially if the knife is designed to have a fine point and the edge blunts it off, are instances.

If the man sets out two identical knives with stag handles and the stag of one is nicer, I still check the edges. Edges equal, I take the better stag, naturally, but I won't trade a bad edge for good looks. I'm sure I have passed up some good blades this way, but everyone is entitled to any harmless whims they can afford. You may prefer the niftier handle material.

Production models are all equal, but some are more equal than others. So look at three anyway, if there are three to look at, and if you don't like any of them, look at more. A knife is peculiarly personal. You spend an awful lot of time with one. And when you need that knife it's always because you have a job for it.

Here's a special limited edition, with the Smith & Wesson name, sterling silver guard and pommel, and an etched blade. This is the Bowie. There will be three other such S&W 1,000-run specials.

Using And Not Abusing Knives

12 A knife—any knife—does its best work while slicing. In this operation, the blade is moved into the work and the edge is drawn along the cut. That's how a knife is used, with exceptions, of course.

Consider all the other cutting tools you have or have used: axe, saw, chisel, gouge, scraper, ice pick or awl—even scissors. Each is put to work with its own characteristic attack, so characteristic that in most cases the name of the cut is the name of the tool, and in few cases is the tool much good for any other cut. One may slice with a properly sharp axe and scrape with a chisel and break up ice with an awl and scribe with an ice pick, but that about covers it.

A knife can do it all, or at least can make all the strokes — chop, saw, scrape, chisel, scribe, stab, and gouge — the others can, but what it does best is slice. Keep that in mind and try to keep your knives slicing and you and they will get a lot more work done.

All the discussion of shape and thickness and length of blade, all the advice about handles and guards, all the concern with point location and straight

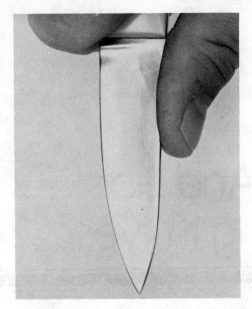

Move the edge into the work and slice. When a sharp edge familiar to your hand through practice is in there, it does all the work.

and curved edges is pointed at keeping a particular knife slicing in the general run of work required by a particular hand: yours. If you require a knife also to stab, or to chop, or to chisel, you can be accommodated in the design. The size and shape you need is already on the market.

The psychologists keep trying to tell us we each have a different experience in this world. For instance, each child in a family lives in a different family than each of the other children in the family. When you choose so intimate a tool as a knife, you bring to the choice your own unique experience and adaptability. I don't pretend to know why or how knife-using skills and prejudices develop, but I do know I do my best knife work with certain shapes, and that with other shapes I must concentrate, unless they are shapes directly suited to the specific work. You and I are doubtless different in most respects, but I am sure we are alike in this.

This is not the place for a discussion of anatomy in detail, even if I were qualified, but it is the place to discuss your hand. You may never have given your

124

hand much thought, though it's been hanging there on the end of your arm all your life. Well, if you're normally constructed and in good health and not too decrepit, your hand can rotate through a considerable arc, it can swing in several directions, and when you combine swings and rotations it can assume a wide variety of attitudes. Since it is attached to your wrist, your wrist governs and controls much of this movement, and since your wrist is part of your arm, and there's an elbow in the middle of that, any work you perform with your hand starts at your shoulder, which is at the other end of your arm and ought to be properly set before your hand starts. You make some of these moves better than others, and your knife should work with your best moves.

You can also change the shape of your hand, from splaying out your fingers to closing your fist and you can make parts of your hand work one way while others go the opposite way. And normally, you don't give any of this a thought — you just stretch out, fumble open the drawer, insert your hand, select the gumdrop you want and pop it in your mouth. It would take the resources of NASA, the Pentagon and General Motors to build a machine to do the same thing and it still wouldn't be worth much as a knife-guidance system.

And perhaps your hand and arms have not yet been worth much as a knife-guidance system. In addition to being truly marvelous in our possession of fingers, hands, wrists, and arms, we are all individual in that possession. They're all different.

If we brought to knife use the same study we bring to Ping-Pong, TV fine-tuning or football throwing, we'd accomplish something. We'd all be pretty good, too. A century ago, most rural Americans knew one end of an axe from the other and some were chopping geniuses. Working with a knife isn't so public as axework, but it's a lot more useful in the twentieth century.

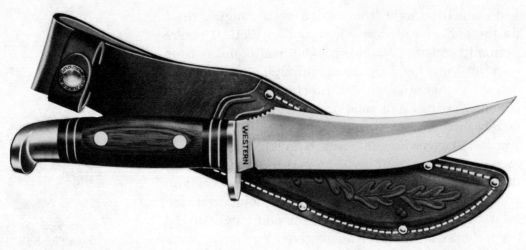

This shape of belt knife is called the buffalo skinner by the romantic people who write ads, and there is some justification. With the thumb rest and the long sweeping edge, this is set up for the long slices. It can do other things, of course, but any new owner who has never had a big, curved-bladed knife before is going to have to learn to use it —carefully.

Good knifework takes a little observation and a lot of practice. The first thing to learn is that if your knife is sharp and your technique correct, you don't need a lot of power. Conversely, if it takes a lot of power, you are either doing it wrong or your knife is dull. Of course, the job of cutting at hand has something to do with it. If you're putting a point on a 2x4 and axe, chisel, and saw are all out of reach, you need an extra-stout knife and good muscle tone.

If you're way behind in knife skills, try whittling sticks between spells on the lawn mower as a steady habit. Whittling is not carving. When you carve, you seek to create some sort of image; when you whittle, you are creating a pile of shavings. But, as the pile grows, the stick you're whittling is sliced into a variety of shapes on purpose and each shaving adds to your skill with the knife.

A more practical exercise is to get whoever buys chickens at your house to buy whole chickens for you to take apart. (The whole chicken is cheaper than the pieces, by the way.) You'll never achieve the lightning speed of the people who take chickens apart for a living, but you can get pretty good at the twelve cuts it takes to make ten pan-sized pieces out of a single bird.

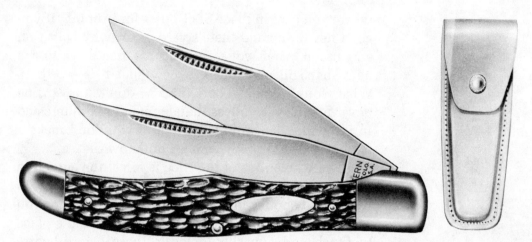

All of us open packages all the time. Try different ways when you can, avoiding the straight power option. Corrugated boxes, for instance, can be slashed in a place or two and then torn apart by main strength and awkwardness. It's slicker and maybe quicker to grasp a thin blade up near the tip—let about 3/8 of an inch stick out—tightly and make a pass along three sides just below the top of the box and tilt it back.

If you've not carried and used a knife a great deal, it will seem time consuming at first to reach in your pocket or around behind on your belt and get the knife out, make the cut and put it back. After a good while, you'll discover you're not thinking about this and the knife appears in your hand and disappears back to safety automatically.

By all means, each time you use a pocketknife, fold it up and put it back in your pocket. You get, as I said, very quick at this. If you set it down, open, so it's handy for the next cut, you will walk away from it and lose it. That's how I lost the last knife I lost. I was helping a fellow tie some stuff down on his car and left the knife in his trunk. Never saw him or the knife again. So put it back, every time.

Practice, practice—even push it a little. Use the knife instead of scissors for clipping the paper, and,

Given a two-bladed knife like this large hunter, where the two blades offer edges about the same length and style, it makes good sense to sharpen each blade a little differently. In this instance, the thinner skinning blade would be edged at a 15° or 20° angle, while the thicker blade is better set up at a 30° angle. Then, the thick blade does most of the chores, and the very keen edge of the thin blade is reserved for times when its extra sharpness is needed. It's a little bit like the splitting-chopping division of labor between the two edges of a double-bit axe.

127

where you can, in place of clippers for pruning. If you get a new knife and there's yard work, why belt it on and use it when you can. The practice at getting a new shape in and out of a new sheath is worth it. What would the neighbors think? I don't know. Mine never mention it, unless they happen to be interested in the particular knife I'm using. If you don't make a big deal out of it, they won't. I do know that.

The whole idea of the slice is to get the edge into the cut and let it do the work. With that clearly in mind, you should look at the job at hand before you put the knife to it. There is a place to start and a place to finish and you should locate these before beginning.

Take, for instance, the seven-bone blade chuck steak (or pot roast) I have just discovered as a cheap beefy dinner. There are two problems with this cut of beef: It has lots of bones and lots of connective tissue in it for one, and it is big for another. With a couple of savvy cuts you can get rid of the biggest bones and at the same time make it small enough to fit in a pan for pan-broiling, or on an ordinary rack for broiling, or down into a Dutch oven for pot roasting.

Which cuts? Well there are two genuine bones in this piece of meat, one maybe 5 inches long and the other 7 inches. You notch away the tissue at the upper end of these, then slip the knife around the end, slicing it along, then tilt the blade to suit the slant of the bone and slice down one side and back up the other. The bone falls out with hardly enough meat on it to interest your dog, who shouldn't have that splintery bone anyway. Do this for both bones, and notch through the fat and connective tissue all around the roast. It will now all fit in a normal pan, and your wife will be very impressed, even if it is rather dangly in parts.

Try, given a suitably thin knife, to get good enough to slice and chop a large onion before you start crying. If you can do two big onions before they

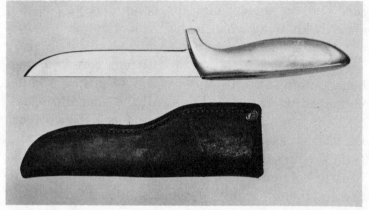

get to you, you are fast. Don't waste time learning to peel potatoes with a knife, however, because the patent peelers are infinitely superior for that job.

Out in the woods with a deer down, you do the same things you have done before, except if you have become more skilled at using a sharper knife you'll find the job so simple you'll wonder where the trouble went. You'll see it as a series of cuts, each made in its own best fashion, making the knife slice most of the way.

I know of a very young fellow who has a passion for deer liver. He hunts with his father, in fact, because the law won't let him hunt alone. Every time they see a successful hunter with a deer, he offers to dress it out in return for the liver and heart and he gets lots of takers. His father helps sometimes because otherwise the job takes this eleven-year-old kid ten minutes.

If all that sounds like I am saying that it's all in knowing how, you have it in a nutshell. Practice will provide the know-how.

If you need an image to work up to, think of yourself at a big family dinner, or at the head of the buffet, with a standing rib roast, a big ham, or a turkey in front of you. And what do your guests see? A sharp knife skillfully dropping delicious meat on their plates, carved with class and dash. That is what they see. You do not get class by being classy. You get class by knowing what the hell you're doing.

So practice.

There's a practice of a different sort you had better follow, also. It is pretty easy to misuse a knife and wind up with less knife. All the guarantees and all the experts say don't use a knife as a screwdriver, crowbar or axe. Still—there's the sudden need for a little prying and you'd rather risk the blade than walk back to the house for a nailpuller, or whatever. I do it myself, though it does depend a little bit on which knife I have in hand. You just can't do much effective levering with a folding knife, and there's not much point in chopping with anything weighing under a half pound, and fiddling with screw slots will take chunks out of nearly any edge.

That sort of misuse has its distinct limitations. It is so self-defeating no one does much of it. There is a subtler kind of misuse you could describe as making the wrong cut in the wrong place. I have seen, for instance, fellows getting very brave with bones when the fact is anyone with any knife ought to be very cautious about bones.

It's time right here for the bolt-cutting story. Every knife maker but Buck says bolt cutting is a stunt, while Buck uses as a company symbol a little sketch of a knife cutting a bolt. The truth is that almost any good knife will cut stove bolts—if you do it right.

I was interested by this a decade or more ago, when Buck's national merchandising effort was just off to a good start. I talked to Al Buck about it, in fact. At the time, bolt cutting was a fairly routine test in the Buck factory, which is doubtless now deservedly far larger than it was then. I think the idea of using this test to sell knives was inspired, but it sure did stir up the animals. The reason it did and does is that you'll tear up almost any knife if you do it wrong.

The right way is: 1. Be sure you have a stove bolt

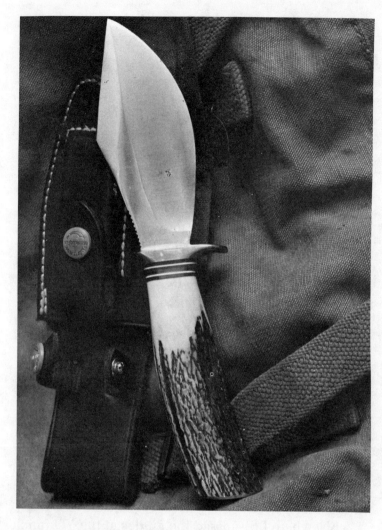

Here's the real belt-knife equivalent of the double-bitted axe. The straight false edge is hatchet-sharp for rough cuts and little chops while the long —for the length of the knife — main edge is knife-keen for slicing. Such design takes practice to use properly, but is quite efficient. For work that takes a fine point, however, there needs to be a pocketknife handy.

and not a hardened machine bolt. 2. Set the bolt on a firm surface, wood for choice. 3. Set the edge of the blade down in one of the threads, and be sure it isn't cross-threaded, so to speak. 4. While holding the blade firmly in contact with the bolt, lightly tap it with a hammer and keep it up. 5. After a while, the knife cuts the bolt.

After Al told me this, I went out in the yard with a bunch of knives and some bolts. I tried every knife at hand on the job, working on a stump, and they all did it and none were damaged. Several of those knives are pictured in this book—an old Morseth, a Randall #7, a Gerber, a Schrade Boy Scout knife are ones I distinctly remember trying.

A couple of months later I was in the shop of a very good knife maker, whose initials are W. D. Randall, Jr., discussing this with the fellows. Bo, I must say, wasn't there. Well, it wound up with me showing them how to do it at their insistence. However, the chap who was doing the tapping grew bored and, in the medium-firm belief I wouldn't lie to him and the solid belief in his own product, gave the blade a hell of a whack about halfway through. The bolt sprang apart in halves, and the blade displayed a sickening half-moon chunk crumpled out of its edge. He had made the wrong cut in the wrong place. I've done the same thing on a chicken and been sorry for it.

Twisting cuts are not good for edges. The forces developed are tremendous and they push exactly the wrong way for the edge to stand it. That fine edge works only if it is backed up by the blade in direct line. If you twist you get the edge out of line with the meat of the blade and it is unsupported. That's why trying to use the knife as a screwdriver will bugger almost any blade going. You know a stubborn screw can tear up a screwdriver if you get it out of line, so don't be surprised at the loss of a knife point or a chip in the edge.

Elsewhere I discussed the guides at the YO ranch who use knives to rip bony pelvises and rib cages open. Why don't they bust edges? They don't twist the blades, that's why. I loaned one of them my Loveless knife for the day's work one time. This is rather a special knife, hollow ground so thin you can ripple the edge — actually see it bend — over your thumbnail (I like the knife very much, but it sure takes knowing to work right). The man ripped three carcasses with no problem.

Most misuse damage messes up the point, I'd guess, and that figures because fixing a busted point sometimes requires major reshaping of the whole blade. The usual blade starts shaping to the point well back, and when the point isn't there anymore you practically have to start over. You never get the same knife back, and the odds are against your being able to finish up with an improvement. This, above all, keeps me cautious with my knives.

The ordinary care of a knife is so simple most of us neglect it. All it has to be is clean and dry—all the time. When it can't be, wipe it off and oil it as often as you can, even if it's stainless. If it's a folding knife, oil the joints regularly; in fact, often.

Special handle materials take special care. Leather shouldn't be left wet, ivory doesn't like changes in climate, and horn cracks against some stresses or just when it gets very dry.

If your sheath is oil-tanned, keep it a little oily with an oily kind of leather dressing. If it's a hard, dry leather, nothing beats shoe polish. And you can choose your own color. Don't leave your knife in its sheath between trips. I do it, but it's a lousy idea, and has cost me the gleam on some blades and the finish on some handles. Some leathers have stuff in them that doesn't like knives.

I suppose what using and not misusing a knife adds up to is: We should stop taking our knives for granted. They are tools we have to learn to appreciate, learn to use, and learn to take care of, even if they have been there all along. There's one sure cure for taking sharp edges for granted — try to get along without one.

Carrying A Belt Knife

13 All the intelligent places to carry a belt knife are behind you, with few exceptions. Whatever else you're carrying on your belt, the belted knife goes behind one hip socket or the other. Hung anywhere in front, your knife could hurt you pretty bad.

The exceptions are rather romantic!

You could wear your knife in your boot. It can be done. This method requires that you wear a boot, of course. With the sheathed knife anchored therein, you get two choices: Tuck your trousers into your boot, which could leave some portion of the knife handle sticking out where it can catch on things, or let your pants hang down covering the knife, which requires you to rearrange your clothing to get at the knife. It's probably no worse than digging out a pocketknife.

A sheathed knife can be hung on a packstrap. Given the right keeper, it could even be hung upside down. Military and paramilitary parachutists often do this on their chute rigs; some carry the practice over to their field packs. Usually the sheath, and sometimes the knife handle, too, is simply taped into place

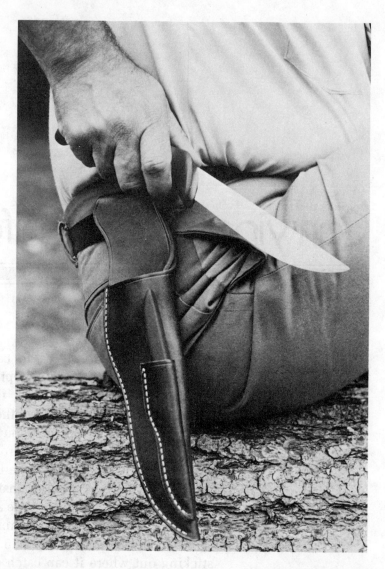

Here's where the leather-sheathed belt knife is worn — behind-the-hip — and how this carry works in the field, whether you carry one or two knives in the sheath. These are Gerbers, and Gerber knives are all available in combination with the little one they call the Pixie. This one in our model's hand is the Magnum Hunter.

with riggers' tape. (The civilian equivalent of that is gaffer tape, which well-stocked camera stores carry. It sticks and it's tough.)

Similarly, and often sensibly, sheaths can be fastened to camera-bag straps and musette-bag covers, or even sewn to or built into handgun holsters — homemade outfits, that is. With the use of Velcro, short sheathed knives can be nailed down inside pants pockets as well as boots. Sometimes knife

136

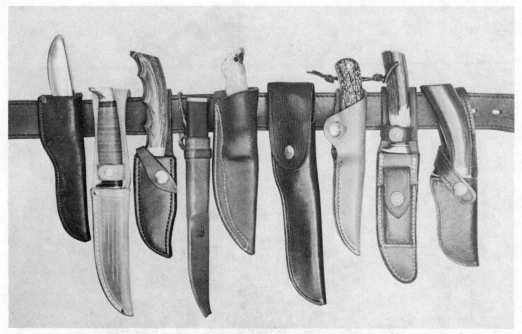

sheaths are built right into pants legs, resembling the rule pocket on American overalls.

Any and all of those techniques work. What doesn't work is a sheathed knife on your belt ahead of your hip socket. Even in normal activity you often bend forward, which points the knife at tender places and/or pokes the end of the handle into other, if less vulnerable, tender places like the short ribs. With a knife belted out front, a misstep that sits you down real fast when the knife has shifted just wrong could drive the blade right into your leg, or even between your legs.

How about all those romantic Arabs and Pathan tribesmen, the fellows with the sashes and the fancy-handled daggers on their tummies? Well, they figured this all out a long time ago and they sheath those knives in metal. Your average Arab sheik takes fewer chances with his out-front anatomy than most. His knife sheath is heavier than his dagger. (Actually, that exotic upturn at the end of the sheath is another

There is not a whole lot of agreement on how a knife should carry. Here are nine, representing a price range of $15 to $150 and no one can make up his mind. The four that hang low make the most sense. The Gerber on the left I cherish and have carried many miles and it dug me in the short ribs once a day like clockwork. I favor the pouch —four of which are shown — rather than the blade-sheath/handle-strap type.

137

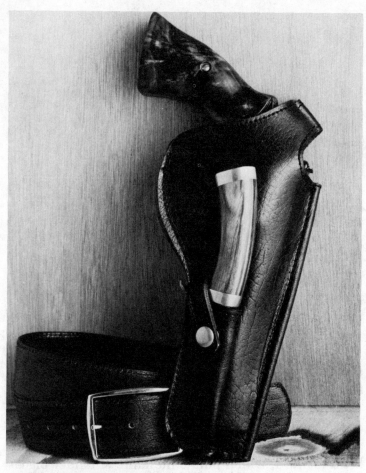

design factor, and not simple Oriental weirdness. What it does is anchor the knife: The upturn hooks under the sash to promote general security and permit a positive draw.)

In fact, almost everywhere that knives are carried on the front of the belt, they are sheathed in metal or wood. The Gauchos and other civilized knife toters of South America do it that way, and so did the Germans with all their dress daggers and bayonets, and likewise most naked or seminaked tribal types, wherever found.

Here, we sheath in leather and we hang the knife out back someplace.

It can, however, get a little complicated. It got so

complicated once that I had a sheath made so it would hang at three heights. That was for a heavy long knife.

Given that a right-side (or left for southpaws) carry is desired, and that the knife is placed behind the hip socket, there are still decisions to be made. There are pouch sheaths and sheaths that cover the blade and strap the handle and there are variations between. The position of the pommel of the handle relative to the belt is what you want to organize to suit your peculiarities.

The all-around champion for comfort and handiness is the Finnish pouch. It swallows the whole knife, just about, so there is no strap to do up—that is important. The sheath itself hangs from a separate belt loop, which puts the whole thing below the belt. It dangles there and feels insecure, but it will dangle for a long time, all the while permitting its wearer to sit, stand, run, bend, and contort. Theoretically, the outfit could jam itself on the other side of a sapling as you went by, or tangle in a fence, but it hasn't happened to me yet.

Next best is a pouch sheath—again, no straps—with a belt loop that puts the pommel right at the belt line. Put such an outfit a little farther around and the only time it annoys you is when you sit down and the point digs in somewhere. Some of those times the pommel will gouge you.

A pouch that carries higher has to be, in my opinion, strapped pretty tight to the body, which eliminates most sit-down problems, but is not quite so handy when time comes to return the knife to the sheath. Clothes get in the way.

It is as important to be able to sheath the knife quickly and conveniently as it is to unsheath it in a hurry. Safety straps with snaps and the like are definite annoyances in this respect. The user will one day sheath the knife without snapping the strap and the result will be a lost knife. That lost knife is built into the future by such a sheath.

Riggers get little pouches like this together for all kinds of equipment in parachute-oriented military outfits. Civilians can manage the same sort of thing in auto seat-cover, sailmaker, upholstery, and similar shops. This one carried this knife a long way.

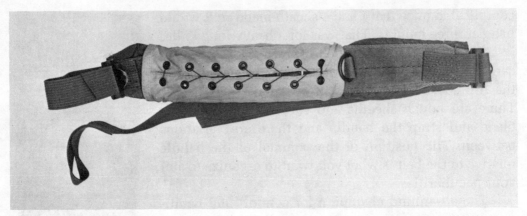

This is a military response to the possible instant need for a knife. The pocket is lashed on the pack or chute-strap and sewn shut with thread through the grommets provided. At need, the user simply snatches it open, breaking the thread, and there's the knife, cleverly lanyarded so if this all happens in the air or while dangling in a tree the knife doesn't answer the call of gravity.

Opposite:

In those societies where knives are worn out front, they are sheathed in wood or metal. From the left: North Africa, South America, Tibet.

A solid "blade" sheath with a good belt loop is OK. Hundreds of thousands of knives are carried in them. The required keeper is an annoyance, of course. The kind that snap around high are awkward; the kind that snap around low sometimes get cut; the type that cross over the guard slanting almost always get cut. That belt loop should be part of the sheath, folded. For comfort, the loop should put the pommel at the belt, but few do. Mostly, they ride higher.

The low-position standard sheath is not a complete delight either. Unless very sturdy, and therefore heavy, such sheaths are weak backed and, after a while, let the point of the knife swing in and the butt lean out. In that condition, you get the worst of both worlds. This doesn't happen when the keeper strap circles the handle up high, but the high keeper is not so handy as the medium and low keeper, particularly when sheathing the knife, and so the high keeper is not usual.

There are all sorts of variations in knife sheaths. There are split pouches that take almost the whole knife, but are snapped together. There are blade sheaths with keepers that cover nearly the whole knife handle. There are "locking" and "safety" sheaths of all manner of design, ranging from wood or plastic linings to snap rigs right on the knife handle. There are metal-bound sheaths, and heavy riveted sheaths.

141

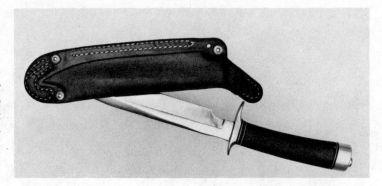

Every once in a while, a holster designer will fool around making a knife sheath, most likely for himself. The result can be something like this. To get one like it, take this picture to a really good holster maker together with your knife and wallet.

There are even upside-down shoulder holsters for knives.

However, any given sheath is either a pouch, into which most of the knife is thrust, guard and all, and held by friction, or it is a blade scabbard covering the blade and with separate features to confine the handle. I have never seen a clamshell knife holster nor have I ever seen a rig that holds the knife parallel to the belt, although I've often thought it would work for a short knife, and might be pretty handy. (I am told one custom knife maker has such a rig.) I have seen split-front spring sheaths for "fast draw," from which the knife is produced just like you get a revolver out of a Berns-Martin holster.

Regardless of design type, a good sheath is stiff. Traditionally, this is accomplished by using several pieces of heavy leather, but how stiffness is obtained is unimportant. This stiffness is the main protection for the personal anatomy, and is very useful when resheathing.

Properly, a sheath should have plugs and welts to position the knife. Along the cutting-edge side of the sheath, there should be a minimum of three layers of leather. The sewing and workmanship should be as good as that found in superior handgun holsters.

Face it: A lot of knives are sold with flimsy blade sheaths, made to carry the knife high to save leather, offering a pair of slits for belt loop, and it is a lot of trouble to find or make another. Such sheaths are OK

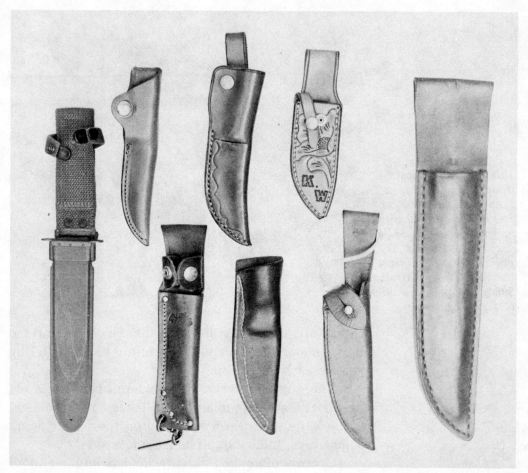

to use if riveted to a board or otherwise nailed down to a web strap or pack frame. They are pretty good protection for a knife to be carried in a pack. But never thread one onto your belt and forget it. Watch it for a few days to be sure it isn't going to bite you.

There are a few more angles to consider. Thus far, we have considered only the problems of a fellow carrying only a belt knife on his pants belt. Most of the time, however, the knife wearer is carrying other things, too. He may be backpacking, which narrows down the belted location to between the pack frame and his hip socket or off the belt entirely. He may have a rifle slung on his right shoulder, which means,

All of these are pretty safe carrying devices. The big sheath on the right is fiberglass lined, and the 10-inch knife it holds is heavy enough to do without a keeper.

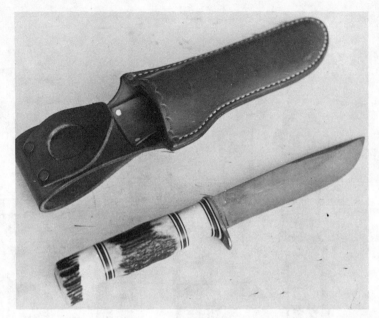

This outfit is the most rational combination of leather and safety around. The sheath is lined with formed fiber and the knife snaps into its socket. The popover keeper works, too. This is a Morseth Safety Sheath, still available on special order.

if his knife isn't under his coat, that he'd best shift the knife inboard or the rifle and knife will be clattering against each other.

The guy who wants to rifle hunt, carrying a big packboard, a handgun and a knife has a real problem. If the knife or sidearm won't go on the pack rigging somewhere, the handgun better ride inside.

Or, very often, he'll be carrying a handgun and no rifle. A confirmed handgunner who also belts a knife will find things easier if he simply decides to cross-draw either the knife or the gun. On the basis that the knife will be used far more often than the gun, I have long opted for the spring cross-draw holster for the sidearm and the ordinary right-side carry for the knife. With different priorities, another fellow might go the other way. For me, a high-carried cross-draw gun is far more accessible than any cross-draw knife arrangement I have seen. Very likely that is the result of having a large, long torso and plain old 35-inch sleeves.

I have also simply hung the knife behind a right-side handgun. In the old pictures, one can see outdoors types with handguns on their right hips and large knives in the middle of their backs, set up diagonally and rather high, which would seem necessary for a horseman. The Finnish pouch sheath for a relatively small knife works well behind a small or medium-sized handgun carried on the right. Neither interferes with the other.

Someday, perhaps, I will marry a knife to a handgun and have some craftsman put up a combination holster-sheath. I haven't yet, and have never seen such a rig, although there is now one on the market. There's a cute little gadget made as an insert for policewomen's handbags that carries a 4-inch .38, some spare ammo, and handcuffs. This will also ride on the belt, so the theory is sound enough. The tremendous variety in knife shape and size prohibits any standard production item, of course.

For the most part, knives are bought together with their sheaths. And they stay with that sheath. That makes the sheath part of the package. In many ways, a somewhat less good knife in a good sheath makes more sense than a superior blade in flimsy leather.

Carrying a knife should be simple: Belt it safely; carry it in the same place all the time; make securing it in the sheath a reflex action, *every time* it is resheathed. You'll have it longer.

You can make out with less-than-ideal leather. This 8-inch Western knife has carried a long way in its lightweight sheath. The high keeper and the low belt position help — it rides much like a Finnish pouch.

Sharper Is Better

14 There are no two ways about it. Putting a superior cutting edge on a knife takes a certain knack. It shouldn't, because the physical accomplishment is slight, but it does. You know you have the knack when your friends bring you their knives to sharpen. And you are especially certain when they bring you knives they have tried to sharpen.

If you're normal, there is a distinct satisfaction in making six or seven passes at the stone with a pal's dull knife and handing it back to him ready to shave hair off his arm. He'll get a funny look on his face because he has worked and worked on that edge and gotten nowhere.

What happens is that he gets it almost right and then waffles back and forth and never quits at the right place. With your knack, you just rip off his irregularities and lay a smooth edge on the established foundation. If you can do it, it's fun.

The physical accomplishment is indeed slight. A keen edge results when two plane surfaces intersect in the center of the blade's edge from heel to tip. There is

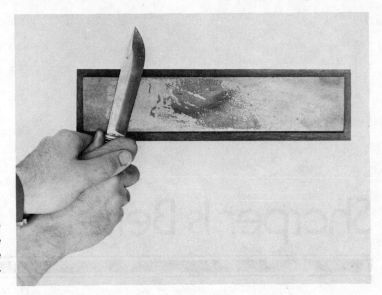

It's simple if you develop the knack. You start here — actually this stroke is already started — and carry the stroke out to the point. The trick is to make all the strokes at the same angle, working in both directions.

no other way to make a knife sharp, barring a bevel edge which merely moves that pair of planes off-center, or a cannel or apple-seed edge, which employs two convex surfaces.

The knack then is in hands that can set up an angle between the blade and the stone and then hold it through a succession of strokes, first on one side and then the other. The hands have to *feel* that pair of planes.

The result is visible, incidentally; you can see it. If there's a clean, bright level ribbon of new surface running along the edge on both sides, the edge is keen or it will be when those surfaces intersect along the full length. Wherever those lines waver or simply don't meet, whether from irregularities in the blade surface or from a changed angle or a hitch in the sharpening stroke, there will be a flat spot on the edge. Looking at the edge — the intersection of the planes—in a good light will reveal this. Obviously, a series of flat spots do not make a keen edge.

The difference from dull to keen is often a matter of one or two-thousandths of an inch or even less either way, which is why just a few passes over the

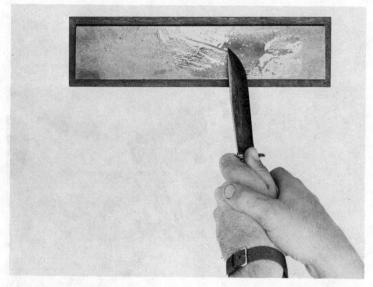

When you get toward the point of most knives, you raise the butt of the knife to keep everything even. After this pass to the right, you make its mirror image, going to the left. The knack includes learning that some shapes sharpen easier for you than others.

stone may finish a botched job properly. All it takes—to risk being repetitious — is to get two flat surfaces intersecting at the edge.

Now, there are many ways to accomplish this. On soft knives, the butcher's steel works fine; again on soft knives, the circular honing motion many people use will eventually produce an approximation of a keen edge. There are appliances to fasten to the blade that will automatically provide the flat intersecting planes that make an edge when the blade is rubbed against the stone. It is possible to hold the knife steady and manipulate the stone.

Any flat surface sufficiently hard and abrasive will serve as a stone, but materials specifically designed for sharpening steel tools are the better choice. There was a time when I knew what was best, but now I don't. The classic answer has been one or another form of Arkansas stone; the mass answer is good old Carborundum; the new answer begins to look like one or another of the space-age materials. My own choices are soft Arkansas or Washita stones.

Regardless which material you use, they are all used alike. By moving the edge across the stone while

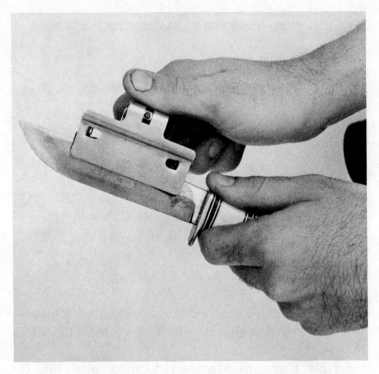

If all else fails, get help from a sharpening guide. This is a Buck Honemaster, which clamps on by spinning a knurled wheel. Razor-Edge is similar, but clamps with set screws. Both work by forcing you to hold the angle.

pressing it down firmly, you abrade the metal. If you do it right, you get those two intersecting planes.

I've watched the man who puts the edges on bench-made Randall knives. He takes the day's production and lays it out in a line, then he gets himself set — good footing and all. Before him is a bench that mounts an 18-inch oilstone, the kind you can rotate in its own oil bath. To get the oilstone below his elbows, he stands on a platform.

Then, one at a time, he picks up the knives, all ground clean to a rough edge. With a firm — really firm — two-handed grasp on the handle, he sets the rear end of the edge down on the oil-wet stone, lifts the back of the blade, and then, in a slicing motion, puts plenty of beef into a stroke along the edge, from heel to point. Alternating sides, working on the coarse side of the stone, he will make perhaps six passes, and look at the edge. If it now runs clean, he flops the stone and takes several passes on the fine side.

The pressure is never let up. Each stroke is full power all the way and the man gets his shoulders into every one. The only difference between a small short knife and a long one is the length of the stroke. Randall, by the way, calls this *honing*.

A high percentage of the blades edged this way in this shop will shave hair from your arm. The two planes that are formed intersect at an angle of about 20°, which is a good average. An angle of 12° or 15° makes for a keen edge, but one that doesn't last as long. A 30° angle can still be sharp, and it lasts a great deal better.

It is all very well to learn that's how to sharpen a knife, you say, but how about you?

Modified however you like to suit your circumstances and equipment, that process is what you must follow unless you use one of the sharpening appliances on the market. In that case, the appliance forces you to follow exactly the same procedure. It is not necessary to use an 18-inch stone; it is not necessary to stand up and get both hands on the knife; it is certainly not necessary to have a special bench for the purpose. I get a lot of knives quite sharp on a hand-held 12-inch stone on the kitchen counter; and there's a 6-inch stone in my desk that works, too.

It is, however, necessary to make whatever arrangement you can that will permit you the full-pressure, full-length stroke at the appropriate angle. You'll find that on a short stone, you'll have to pull the blade toward you faster, making the stroke move more along the edge than across it. You may find your setup works best with the stone's narrow side toward you while you push and pull through the sharpening strokes.

On most knives, as you get closer to the point, you'll have to lift the handle some to maintain the angle at the edge on the curve. How much you lift depends, of course, on the particular knife you are working. Your eyes can tell you how you're doing on

Left:

There are several varieties of this carbide hone on the market. It can be used as a steel is used, or, if you must, you can treat the flat surface as a stone. Works, too. These have gotten quite classy of late, but I like old ones like this for their useful wedge shape.

Right:

Gerber's got up this kit, which is pretty useful. There are two double-faced stones, some good oil, and a cloth in a convenient box. They throw in a wedge with which you can check your blade angle.

this after three passes, each side. You want the new surfaces to stay about the same width all the way.

The rule is to alternate strokes on each side of the blade. Don't be doctrinaire about it, though. If one side gets ahead of the other, give the slow side a few extra licks. The same is so when part of the edge falls behind, as might happen with a small stone and a big knife. It is also entirely OK to work half the edge at a time to save gear-shifting, so to speak, in the middle of the stroke. However, you have to lap the "joint" carefully and be sure your angle stays the same fore and aft. Don't finish half the blade and then try to meld the other half. Carry them along together, alternating equal sets of strokes.

Don't, with a good, tough knife, waste your time taking light "finishing" strokes. Without your exerting heavy pressure on it, the stone doesn't cut. If you get into postgraduate edging technique and get a really fine stone for the last strokes, don't let up the pressure. You still have to bear down to get any abrasion.

Remember *always* that you are leaning very hard

on a very sharp tool. Keep your hands out of the way and don't let anyone stand close, particularly children. A kid can beat you to the draw every time at sticking his hand in quickly where it isn't wanted.

A firmly nailed-down stone is a distinct benefit. You can chuck it in a vise, put cleats on the benchtop, tape its box to the table, fasten the box to a board and C-clamp it down on a counter — try anything along that line. It is possible to do the job one-handed while you hold the stone with the other, but it's difficult and you don't get so good a result. And make a serious error and you could cut the stone-holding hand badly.

There should be some liquid medium on the stone's surface to float the microscopic chips away. You can touch up an already fair edge on a dry stone if you're in a hurry, but you'll have the chips to deal with next time. What medium? Light oil—even "honing" oil — is best, but saliva (plenty), salad oil, and automotive oil also work. For all I know, liquid soap or hand lotion would work fine. Have plenty of whatever on the stone when you're finished so when you wipe it off, you clean the stone. If a stone gets really cruddy, get plenty of detergent into hot water and scrub it thoroughly. Also rinse it thoroughly and then find a nice warm place for it for several days so it dries thoroughly.

Let's say you have all this stuff and you take what you've read so far and try hard and it doesn't work. You determine, in fact, that you don't have the knack. You get a wiggly edge, or can't bear down hard enough, or the whole procedure bores you or whatever—and yet you still want sharp knives.

Well, man is a tool-using animal and all you need is another tool. Obviously, if you worked out a way to get two-point contact on the stone, you would be able to hold the angle that will produce the sharp edge. For a single knife, you could cobble up some spacers to tape on each side to give you the correct angles. Then you'd just have to lay the edge and the spacers

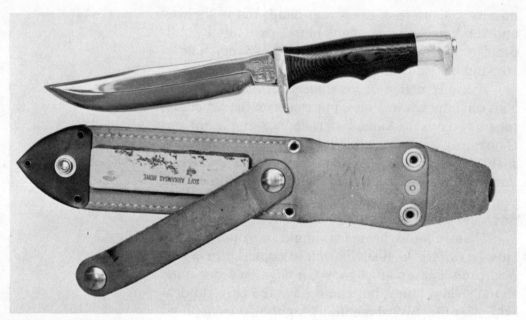

Epoxying a thin Arkansas stone to the back of a sheath isn't a bad idea. This one, with leather strap cover, appeared on some Loc-Knives.

on the stone and grind away. You could experiment with Scotch tape and cardboard.

For more than one knife, get a sharpening appliance. The best-known one is called Razor-Edge. (Buck offers a similar device.) It buckles onto the back side of your blade with set screws, and then you do exactly what the Razor-Edge instructions tell you to do, which is exactly what you've been told to do here free-hand: Grind hard and produce a pair of planes intersecting at the edge. The difference is that a properly adjusted Razor-Edge won't let you do it any way but right. The drawbacks are quite minor. It takes longer to set up each blade with the Razor-Edge. You have problems with the curve and the point until you acquire the knack of the Razor-Edge. The gadget itself costs a few bucks. But compared to otherwise having to put up with dull knives, these are no drawbacks at all.

There are more exotic ways to edge a knife, of course. The foot-pedaled large grindstone, turning slowly with a wet surface, is fine. There used to be—

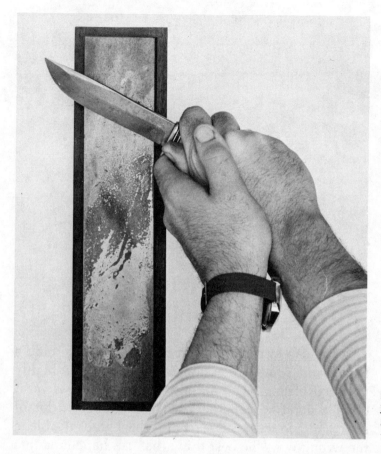

You may find a push-pull stroke more useful for you, even on the big stone. If so, you're in good company, for several top professional knife makers do it that way.

in my childhood—fellows who went around the city sharpening knives in the street with these. They could cut new bevels, then edge them, quickly. There are a precious few left, but they use trucks and automotive power rather than foot power.

Electric grinders are out. Some of the best grinding technicians in the business are custom knife-smiths and they won't even try to use grinders for edging. You can, however, use a belt sander if you have good hands—it is one way to put the apple-seed (convex) edge on a knife. The apple-seed or cannel edge is both strong and long lasting. Buck knives are delivered with such an edge, put on by some form of sander. It lasts, but is nearly impossible to duplicate using a flat stone.

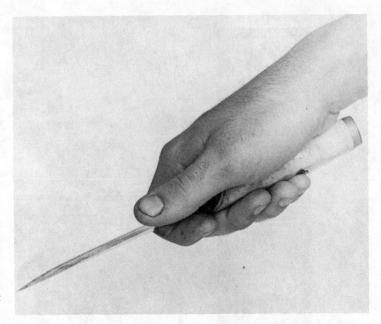

You can also buff an incredibly keen edge onto a blade, and some professionals do it on their highly polished blades. Such an edge is most impressive. It takes a good wheel, the right compounds, a lot of skill, and a lot of practice. If the wheel grabs the blade the wrong way, the best thing that can happen is that you'll be picking a battered or broken knife off the floor, happy the wheel didn't throw the blade through your leg. The best man I know at this took the trouble to rivet a number of steel plates onto his leather apron when he decided to try it on a regular basis.

When working on a belt sander or buffer, you put the edge in backwards, working from the back down to the edge. On a stone, even the big slow-turning wheel, you work from the edge into the blade, as if you were trying to slice layers of stone. It is useful with some shapes of blade to begin your stroke at the tip and push back to the heel.

Butchers use steels to keep edges sharp while they're working. Basically, this is a technique for softer steel than is found in the usual belt knife. A few

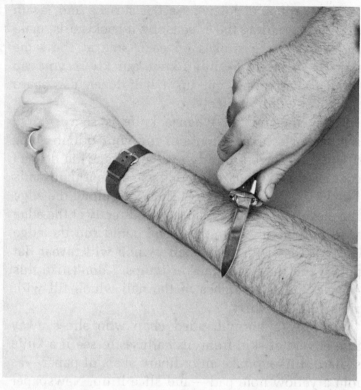

strokes along the steel, which is a sort of cylindrical file, straightens out whatever part of the sharp edge has begun to waver. The steeling happens almost automatically, little time is lost, and the edge stays the same through the whole job. However, butchers are about the best customers for knife-sharpening services, which use stones to make a new edge, and very few household cutting jobs should faze a good edge in midjob. The steel isn't necessary.

I have never personally found a satisfactory way to put a good edge on any hooked blade, such as a pruning knife or hawkbill. There is a way to do it, doubtless, and it will come to me. For now, I use a cylindrical stone and rock the edge over it.

When you're pretty well finished with your edge and you want to refine it, use cardboard as a hone. Almost any cardboard, such as the backs of yellow legal pads, has about the right abrasive quality. Just

157

put the cardboard down on a flat surface and, again with pressure, drag the edge along it backwards, making two or three strokes on each side at the same angle. If you want to dull a knife quickly so you can practice sharpening, cut up a half-dozen cardboard boxes. They'll do it nicely.

How do you tell when a knife is sharp? First, assume a wise expression and run your thumb along or tap your fingers lightly on the edge. This doesn't accomplish anything until you have done it thousands of times, but it is obligatory. Then look along the edge for a clean pair of edge planes, and directly at the edge to see if there are flat spots. You could run the edge lightly across your thumbnail, which will reveal flat spots when the edge grabs or jumps. I don't like this because it puts scratches in the nail which fill with grime and look dirty.

I know a horny-handed chap who slices away little slivers of skin from his calluses to see if a knife is sharp. I like to take an ordinary sheet of paper—as from a yellow note pad—and slice it up. Newspaper will do. Of course, if you don't handle a knife pretty well, this isn't much of a test. If you do slice nicely, and the paper grabs or tears, there's probably a dull spot. Any knife worth having can have an edge on it that will ribbon up a sheet of newspaper or mimeo paper. I have owned several very satisfactory knives that will do this handily, and do their work very well, but with which I have thus far been unable to pass that most *macho* test of all—shaving hair.

Shaving is very impressive when done with a knife. Once I had to shave for real with a knife. Happily, I don't shave much of my face and it was a very sharp knife. Usually, a knife that shaves hair does it on the male arm or on the back of the hand. What you do is present the hairy spot to the blade and shave it. Either the hair cuts or it doesn't. If you're smart, you'll cheat by slicing the blade as you shave with it. You'd be surprised how many edges that

Left:
This is an excellent beginning to find on an over-the-counter knife.

Right:
This is a most unusual heavy-bevel buffed edge, as found on Track knives. It surely makes the over-the-counter knife sharp.

Left:
This is a buffed edge with no visible lines and very difficult to photograph. The shiny side of the blade runs right to the edge and stops.

Right:
This is a bad edge on an over-the-counter knife. I wouldn't buy this one if I had a choice. It can be fixed, but why have to bother?

An extreme example of a spoiled edge that ruined itself by rusting out. To fix it would take a major remodeling of the blade. To a microscopic degree, at least, any straight carbon steel edge can do this.

won't shave hair razor-fashion will do so while slicing. I'm not sure how important a shaving edge is, but I know that such an edge really impresses the crowd.

You will hear the uninformed say they don't like their knifes to be too sharp. They're wrong. Give any such person really sharp knives to work with and he will discover after a while that it's dull knives that are dangerous. Sharp ones go where they're supposed to with a lot less muscle behind them. There's this: Incautious cutting habits are soon avoided. And a little blood might flow before the user learns that a knife need not be forced through by might and main.

Sharper is better—you'll see.

How About Buying A $100 Knife?

15 People do it, and maybe they should, but they don't need it. Actually, the heavy price tag is not an automatic rip-off, not in a bench-made knife. In fact, if you had bought $500 worth of $100 knives five years ago, you'd own $1200 to $2500 worth of $100 knives today. No, they don't breed. They appreciate, some more than others. Some of these formerly $100 knives are worth $1000 today. Honest.

However practical the idea of making money is, this is supposed to be a practical look at knives as knives, so we'll lay off collector economics. Bench-made knives themselves are worth the looking.

There are many definitions for bench-made knives. Few of them satisfy me, or fit all bench-made knives. Randall makes good knives in a shop with over a dozen workers; Bill Moran has always worked by himself; some work with apprentices. Randall and Moran both do their own heat-treating; Bob Loveless hires his out. And between Randall and Moran there is a wide technology gap. Randall has gas furnaces, pyrometers, industrial oil baths; Moran has a fire in a

The hand of the maker is the key ingredient in a bench-made knife. This hand is Bill Moran's and the knife is a hunter with a rosewood handle and coin-silver mounts, an individual creation.

charcoal forge, a bucket of water, a lot of direct personal experience, and a good eye. Loveless would say there is a wide technology gap between his shop and the other two, for that matter. He works in sophisticated alloys; his manner of working is totally different; he makes many more knives than Moran and many fewer than Randall.

Regardless of their private opinions of each of the others' work, each of these men agrees that each of the others makes sound bench-made knives. And so do I.

They do have one thing in common, I know for sure: Each makes his own knife. Their patterns are unmistakable. The knowledgeable can identify a Randall or a Loveless or Moran design from across a room by their shapes alone, whether or not they have ever seen the particular model before. But the world being what it is, that knife seen at close range may prove—equally unmistakably—to have been made by someone else. A lot of pretty good bench-made knives are made in imitation of the design leaders' productions.

If imitation is the sincerest form of flattery, then Bo Randall, Bill Moran, and Bob Loveless are three of the most flattered men walking. There are some quite excellent craftsmen who simply don't make knives of their own design. There are more who make one, or two of their own designs and fill out their catalogs with copies. And there are, of course, some fellows who make their own designs, but are not very good designers.

There are now literally hundreds of men—and a woman or several, too, probably—seriously marketing handmade knives. The quality of this production varies a great deal more than the pricing. It seems, these days, that any fellow who takes the time to put together his own blade, a handle, and a sheath figures it's worth $50, or more. Now, $50 or $75 is a lot of money, but have you noticed those bolt-action rifles? The $125 items are now $225, and there are plenty of $400 and $500 models on the market. The dollar isn't what it was, so maybe it makes sense. However, price is no guide in a custom knife.

Ten years ago, you bought a bench-made knife to get an individual design, to get a better and a better-looking knife, and—let's agree on this—for a little snob appeal, a little something special on your hip. Now you buy one, if you buy one, to keep up with the famous Jones family, or because you don't give a damn about the Joneses but want something different.

What you should get in a bench-made knife is the hand of the maker. The knife should be unmistakably craftsmanlike in every respect. For example, some very advanced collectors prefer better craftsmen to deliver the knives unpolished; that is, finely finish-ground only. That way, they can see what the work-man was up to, really see how good he is. Too, polished grind lines are never so sharp as the un-touched lines.

However, you should also get in a bench-made knife what any good production-line knife delivers: a

This little deer sticker was made by R. H. Ruana. He made them all with cast handles and stag insets. Others have finished their knives better, but I never heard one claim he made a better knife for knife work.

163

Little touches, the decorations tradition permits, are often found on bench-made knives. Bill Moran crenellated this pommel with saw and file.

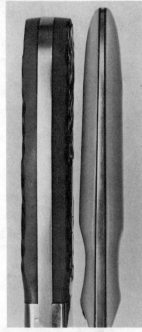

At left is the favored full-tang design, with all sorts of advantages imputed to it. The real class operation these days, however, is the tapered full tang at right. It's a lot more work and you can even see it with the knife sheathed.

straight knife with a straight edge. And that is not so simple as you might think. There are lots of ways a knife can be crooked. For instance, the blade, particularly a forged blade, it seems, can be bent or curved across the flat, warped so the point goes right or left. This was common in thin working knives fifty and more years ago. Poor workmen still manage it today, of course, during heat-treatment.

One way bench-made knives get crooked is when the handle is mounted on a cast, relative to the blade. It happens often and is the sure mark of the unfinished craftsman. You see it best from behind the butt. When the blade—both edge and back—and the handle are not in line, it is obvious.

I have seen knives offered for sale, or proffered as samples, where the pommel had one tilt, the guard an opposite tilt, and the blade yet another. I asked one fellow about this and he asked me what I expected in a handmade knife. Well, I expect straightness first. There is an analogy in the arts: A painter who can draw a perfectly representational cow may try, for me, to create triangular symbolic cows with orange peels —he may pull it off; a painter who cannot draw a cow that looks like a cow is not a painter or an artist and the hell with him.

164

Another crook is when the edge is not in the center of the blade, and a worse is when the edge starts on one side of center and wanders to the other. These are grinding faults; they are occasionally made inevitable by sloppy forging.

It doesn't happen often, but such faults do appear in nicely shaped, slickly finished handmade knives. So, if you're looking over the work of any knife maker, no matter who, check for them. Look at every knife front and back, top and bottom, first — the profile is only part of it. Double-check for them when fit and finish are sloppy. And if you find them, don't buy. A good craftsman won't let anyone see such stuff, let alone offer it for sale.

It really doesn't matter how a knife is made and

Here are some old names in bench knives. From the top: Draper, Ruana, Olsen, and Morseth. All these knives are fifteen years old. The Olsen is from the early custom production before the Olsen knives sprouted guards and pommels. The Morseth was made by Harry Morseth himself. All are representative early bench-made knives, bought to use, not collect.

A raft of knife makers is floating around out there now and keeping up with them is a full-time job. This Cajun knife is, I am told, a pretty fair knife these days. It is finished and fitted to a degree very few met in the early days. Apart from an increased craft ability, there are new machines at work, and a greatly increased public awareness of quality.

there are conflicting opinions on such basic questions as hardness, the importance of rust-resistance, and hilting technique. By whatever method, good men make good knives, which is why method doesn't matter. There are differences, of course, and we'll discuss some of them.

The two big breakdowns are between them that forges and them that grinds. And the blacksmiths are losing ground. Most bench-made knives are ground out of the basic bar these days. There are still those who heat the steel and beat it to shape, however, and some of them are among the best.

Forging is an economical way to push steel into shape. You get more knife for less stock, but it's a whole lot more complicated than just grinding away what you don't want. Now, the fellows that forge get used to the fire, and so they often do their own heat-treating. The grinding men, on the other hand, get very, very good at refined shapes, but they generally send the blade out for the hot work.

I think you get a good knife either way. The forging is more romantic; if the smith does his own heat-treating, you get more of the hand of the maker; if his heat-treating technique isn't so good, you could get trouble, too. The stock-removal people can concentrate on what is admittedly a more precise method.

Steel is not all that simple. Smiths who forge a lot find a billet now and again that goes where it wants to go. That is, they can be working on a straight blade and wind up with a skinner. Forging being the mystic effort that it is, most of them run such a billet out to a curve and throw another in the fire.

If you want a knife with a lot of curve in it, you're more likely to get it from a man who forges. It's as easy as pie for him to take ¼x1¼-inch bar stock and forge out a 1½-inch wide, relatively thin blade with a long curve and a high point. If he does it right, the resulting knife is a good, tough blade. If it's the right kind of alloy, one he has worked with for a long time,

166

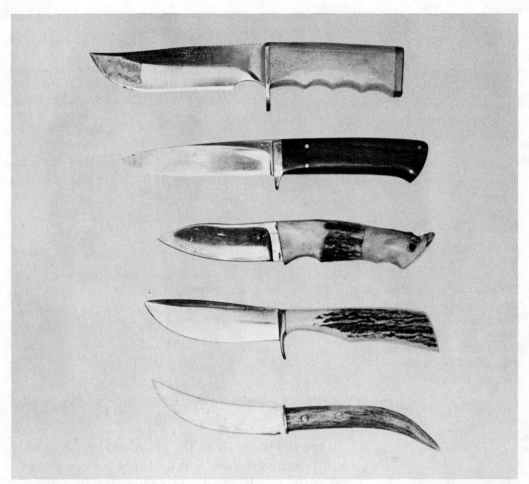

his one-blade-at-a-time heat-treating will get you the physical characteristics you want. It's a truism, by the way, that men who forge their knives don't change steels at the drop of a new idea. There's another truism—most fellows who forge take the heat-treated blade and rap the anvil good and hard with it. This stroke on the back of the blade will break it if there's a flaw in it.

The stock-removal artist who wants a point an inch above the back of a 1½-inch wide blade has to start with stock 2 inches wide. He has to worry about what knife people call the "grain" of the bar, too. To get it to run about right through the curved blade, he

The Seguine at the top is the size the average custom knife used to be. The other four, a Bone, a Loveless, a Lile, and a Moran, are more typical of 1976 designs. The Moran, actually, is a knife Bill Moran carried himself and I conned him out of.

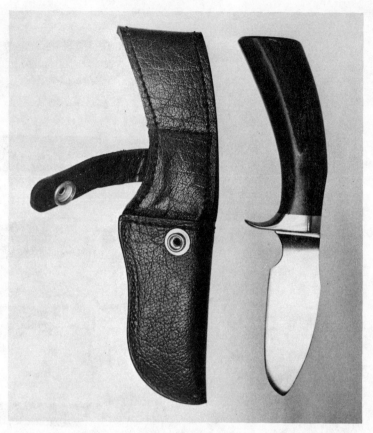

The blunt tip of this Heritage knife reflects the experience and beliefs of Sid Bell, an old Alaskan hand. Points, he thinks, get in the way. This knife is single-purpose, designed to take the hides off meat animals and turn them into packable pieces.

has to run the blade along the grain and let the handle go a little across the grain. It probably isn't important, in terms of handmade knife economics, but there's some wasted steel.

Remember, we're talking about a curved blade and few popular knife designs have curved blades. Most such needs are met by straight knives with curved edges. The majority of good knife designs are straight, and there's no preference one way or the other in practical terms between forged blades and those ground from the bar. Regardless of how the makers themselves grouse about "medieval metallurgy," "blacksmiths," "anybody can grind" and "store-bought heat-treatment," and regardless of their catalog pitches for their own techniques, they all know a good man makes a good knife.

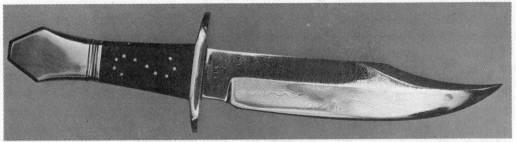

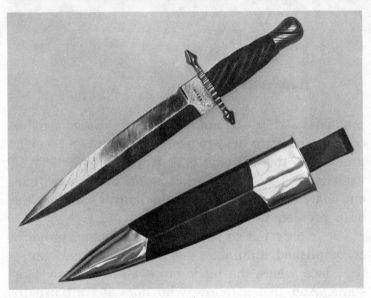

Above:

Today's bench-made knife can be very, very expensive, like this Moran Damascus-steel Bowie worth a pretty good man's wages for a month. It takes Moran nearly a month to make one, with its 512 layers in the blade and immaculate finishing. It takes him several days to make the sheath such a knife deserves. Why a sheath? Moran doesn't make any knives that won't do the job and a sharp tough knife has to have a sheath.

Left:

You do see some curious things in the bench-made knife trade. This marvelous dagger by Moran could be easily tucked into a good museum's collection of prime 500-year-old weapons, but the sheath looks nineteenth century to me.

The bench-makers set great store these days by the full-tang handle as the strongest way to make a knife. I take nothing from them by noting here that the full tang is also the most difficult and time-consuming way to make a handle, particularly when carried to the point of providing integral guard and pommel. It has some undeniable theoretical advantages, but its principal virtue, I am convinced, is that it puts a lot more workmanship on display.

There are, incidentally, some technical disadvantages to the full-tang handle. For instance, there is no way to keep the exposed tang surfaces from discoloring unless they are stainless steel or, to compound the matter fearsomely, the craftsman wraps the surfaces with brass or nickel-silver. A narrow tang beats that

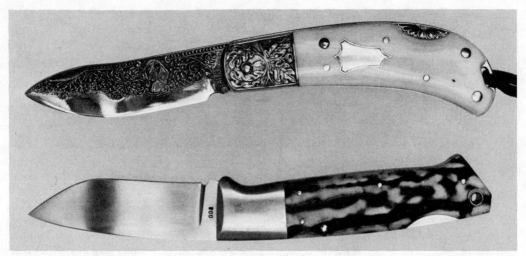

Bench-made no longer means just belt knives. These two folding knives — blades are about 3 inches — were made by hand by men working alone in their own shops. That fine stag-handled stainless-steel hunter model is by Horn, and you could buy fifty ordinary pocketknives for what it's worth. That is hard to believe, I know, so let me tell you the other knife is a Henry Frank knife and you could buy a gross of ordinary pocketknives for what it's worth. Both are lock-blade knives and you have never seen handsomer. At those prices, of course, they are more artifacts than tools, although I have cut things with both of these and they're good knives.

problem handily—by not having any exposed steel, of course. The crafty way to beat the balance and weight problem in the full tang is to taper the tang! That in itself is another whole grinding session, more time, and more cost. It works, but the narrow tang has the basic problem beat for openers.

It is only fair to say that the full tang, properly accomplished, eliminates one theoretical weak spot— the place where the blade stops and a narrow tang starts. And that a fellow who does it well usually makes a knife that people notice. Bench-made knives are noticeable. The blade grinds and shapes are individual; the detailing in matters like the guards is handsome; the sky and your pocketbook form the limits on handle materials.

The knife makers profess—probably in sincerity — that Micarta, a plastic, makes the best handle. Certainly, it is the toughest and most stable material generally available with a good feel. And using it takes a lot of hassle out of the knife makers' existence, because India stag, good exotic wood, ivory, various horns, and *oosic* are very tough to find in good quality and quantity, and they are far more chancy to work with. (What is *oosic?* Why it's walrus penis and a great material for handles. Ask any Eskimo.)

Personally, I find natural materials more pleasing than Micarta, with the exception of ivory. Stag horn and good wood are preferred in the absence of, say, bighorn sheep horn. Ivory is gorgeous and it feels good, but it is terribly heavy and it cracks. The marketplace, should you want to sell a knife, greatly prefers the natural material over the manmade, and really grooves on *oosic*.

The bench-made knife comes with the better sheath most of the time. This is quite important for a blade you're going to use and carry. Most makers construct each sheath individually for the knife at hand, and they make it of the best leather they can lay their hands on. The sheaths are in fact as distinctive as the knives.

And then there's the big question: Are the bench craftsmen turning out better blades than the factories? The answer has to be "yes, they are" when you're talking about the accepted craftsmen. The bench-made knife can be expected to be tougher, sharper, and prettier. If it isn't, don't buy it.

Steel is steel. In the basic business of a knife, you get only auxiliary benefits from magic alloys over any good grade of high-carbon tool steel properly heat-treated. That is, plain high-carbon steel can get so tough, so ideally hard, so sharp that any improvement is marginal on the one hand or theoretical on the other.

But—and it is a big but—the guy making knives one at a time does not have tolerances. If he's worth dealing with, he is doing the best he can every time he comes out of the box. He has decided how his knives should behave, and he has the time to make them do it. The factory dealing in thousands of dozens of knives a month would go broke if it tried to extract the maximum from the materials. Its craftsmen —production-line guys—are fantastic. Check fit and finish on any batch of front-line pocketknives if you don't believe that. The people who put them together

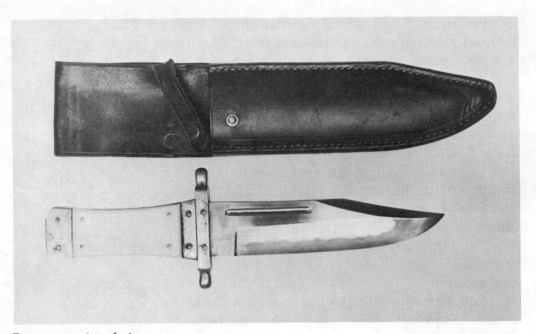

From one point of view, this might be the ultimate in the bench-made knife. It was produced after World War II by the great Japanese swordmaker In- ami. Mounted with great slabs of ivory and coin silver, it still displays the tempering colors along its edge, as does a good Japanese sword. The man who had this made was permitted to see some of the work in progress, and says they treated the job as if it were serious work and not a samurai Bowie knife.

are doing dozens an hour. The technical facilities are tremendous, because if anything goes wrong, it costs real money — try calculating the cost of 5,000 blades spoiled in heat-treatment, for instance — but even the high state of the factory art requires leeway.

So there are tolerances. And tolerances stack one way and then the other. The factories must permit this; the custom knifesmith does not. His knife will sharpen to keenness easier, and will stay sharp longer, than the factory product.

Whether or not the difference makes any differ- ence to you is your problem. When some superiority goes with the hand of the maker and with distinctive design and use of materials, the case for the hand- built knife can be made.

You Could Make Your Own

16 Nearly anyone can make a functional knife for belt carry. Hardly anyone can also make that functional knife good looking. There are three ways to go about this: Make a knife from materials you locate, from scratch, as it were; make a knife from a kit you buy; alter an existing knife or tool to suit your purpose. The latter, while not exactly "making" a knife is close enough for the purposes of this chapter.

Custom knife makers fabricate blades in two ways —stock removal, which means they take an oversize bar and grind away what they don't want; or forging, which means beating red-hot metal into shape. If you already know how to forge, you're in good shape. Most home-grown knives are made by stock removal.

Blade material is everywhere. Saw blades, power hacksaw blades, files, big chisels, any big enough high-carbon tool will do. In his catalog of fine knives, W. D. Randall, Jr. used to detail just how a good knife could be made. He favored forging and so recommended leaf springs from automobiles. Rotary mower blades probably make good knives. Almost any piece

Working slowly and carefully in a first-class shop, an amateur made this pair of knives. He knew just what he wanted and pulled it off. The process was simplified and complicated by the fact that these blades are not steel, but Stellite. They needed no heat-treatment, but they didn't grind very fast. Handle material is ivory Micarta. Harry Archer did the work in Loveless's shop and the left one — Archer #2 — is mine. Harry kept #1. We haven't decided about Stellite as blade material yet.

of tool steel will do. You could even take the remarkable step of buying a suitable piece from a machine shop.

With the blade material in hand and the shape sketched, there is another problem to solve before you can start work: How hard is what you have? If it is already hardened and you are willing to go slow with the grinding to avoid having to reheat-treat your knife, you simply grind away what you don't want. If you'd rather work soft steel, then you must anneal what you have, which simply means you must heat it red hot quite through—no hotter—and then let it cool slowly. If you start with a piece of steel from a mill, it should be soft already.

Before you grind, your piece of steel has to be marked to show not only the outline, but the grind lines, and not only the blade shape, but the handle requirements.

That brings up — somewhat out of place — a discussion of handles. There are several possibilities: You can make a full tang handle, fitting slabs on either side and riveting or bolting through; you can make a narrow tang handle, which means boring a hole full length through the chosen handle material and then using a nut on the threaded end of the tang to hold it all together; you can lash up a bastard rig, epoxying a short tang between two pieces of handle material and maybe adding a thoughtful rivet or two; you can merely shove a short narrow tang back into a hole full of epoxy.

So you have to think about that.

While you're at it, think about a guard. If you do install a guard, it very nearly has to go on over the tang and butt solidly up against the back end of the blade, and a little delicate soldering at the join would not be amiss. (You get the square hole in the tang by drilling round holes close together and then filing them out square.)

Starting with blades like these from Indian Ridge Traders, some rosewood and rivets and a few evenings could result in a nice knife kit for most hunting work.

With the guard and handle questions settled, you go back to the blade and start removing stock. If you are working soft steel, and you are good with files and have good files and a good vise, you can get along without a good grinding wheel, but you can't get a hollow grind. Otherwise, get a grinder, good gloves, good light, and start learning. Most of the knife makers I have watched grind do most of the work long ways of the blade. They get the blade across the wheel only toward the end of the job, or when hollow grinding.

As a matter of fact, if you're not very used to metalworking, it probably would have been a good idea to start with two blade blanks. That's one to ruin and one to finish.

Hack on, then, until what you've got is what you want. As a matter of purist theory, most knives look better if the line of the top of the handle runs as a straight line with the top line of the blade. That means that your guard has to be buried in the handle, which is only practical in some form of narrow-tang design. To get a guard onto a full-tang design requires very careful fitting and then a couple of pins, unless you

A fellow in California named Jones used to furnish knives like this one for $3 and $5. It's shaped out of a big piece of metal-cutting saw, ground to shape, and very roughly beveled. Then, knowing how to cast aluminum, he just dropped a narrow tang into a mold and poured. The result is a rough but serviceable knife that isn't bad looking. If you can cast aluminum, which apparently pours at a temperature that doesn't ruin tempered steel, you could do the same. No, I don't know where Jones is now that we need him.

are one of the world's great solderers. (This description keeps getting ahead of the work. Of course, you don't mess around with handles and guards until you have the blade all hardened again.)

You will have noticed there has been not the least suggestion here of how to apply the heat to anneal the steel in the first place, nor will there be much advice on heat sources for the tempering process. Welding equipment, a heavy-duty propane torch, a charcoal fire with a fan on it—all these will work.

So, with a blade nearly finished, but not with any razor edges on it, you take it up to bright red heat—evenly—and then quench it. Room-temperature water is just fine. Plunge the blade in, and then swash it around. After the quench, you have a very brittle blade. Don't drop it.

The next stunt is tempering. In essence, you have used heat to make your blade as hard as it can be. Now you are going to use less heat to soak the brittleness out of it. For this, you need a bright spot on the blade, which you can only get by grinding, since a file won't touch what you have. The bright spot will change color as you—again evenly—heat the blade. It will get light blue, then straw-colored, and right about there is where you stop and set the blade down somewhere where it will cool out slowly and evenly. Some say the temper is just right when you can just cut the blade with a new file.

Now, you are into the finishing phase. You can fine-grind and sand and polish the blade to its final contours, working one side and then the other evenly. It is probably more important that you get clean lines in about the same place on the two sides than that you get all the lines where you want them. Be sure to keep the blade square with the tang, which will help keep you from grinding crookedness into the knife.

It is quite all right to create the final edge bevels at this stage, but it isn't necessary to do the final sharpening. If you can't resist, go ahead and see if you can make it shave hair. Either way, you should now tape the blade — edge and point and all — and get going on the rest of it.

The first thing to do is square off the blade at the tang. This is the butt of the blade, against which the guard will rest in a narrow-tang design. In a full-tang outfit, naturally, you'll have to take the entire outside to nearly finished profile, then decide how much tang you need and whether or not you need to take it full length.

The truth is, most of us choose the blind tang at this point and therefore shorten the tang down to half or two thirds the length of the handle. However, if you're anxious to go full length, decide how much total handle you need and cut the tang at that length —or a little longer. You now face threading the tang. That means locating the right die and a nut to go with it. You'll need a washer — a big one to be a flat pommel or a little one to go under the countersunk nut. Some makers drill and tap a big piece of brass or aluminum or whatever to thread onto the tang as a combination pommel and tang nut.

Now fit the guard by cut and try. Ideally, it should fit tightly, but solder covers small gaps. Before soldering, polish the surface toward the blade. It is difficult to do this later on. Of course, check the squareness of the outfit before you solder.

If you're going to fit spacers, now's the time to select and prepare them and fit them behind the guard.

You must drill the handle material now. Don't try, of course, to shape the handle. Just be sure you can get the shape you want from the available material. If you're going with a blind tang, don't try to fit the tang too tightly into the hole. Rather leave enough room to keep the handle square to the blade. That means you have to create some sort of lash-up to hold it while the epoxy sets up. With all square and ready to tighten up, daub the hole full of adhesive and lash it up.

In the case of the full-tang and long-narrow-tang

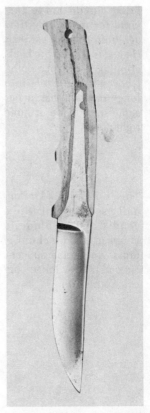

I'm not sure you could construct a narrow-tang knife in more workman-like fashion than this. The hole leaves room for the epoxy, but fits tightly around the ricasso. The tang is tapered, with no sharp corners, eliminating any weakness where tang meets blade. Who was the workman? Bob Loveless, a professional.

177

Ernst Gaydn made this knife for me a long time ago from a sheep skinner. He just reground the back, clipping it to form a point. I haven't seen Ernie in a long time, but I bet he has some such blade at hand right now.

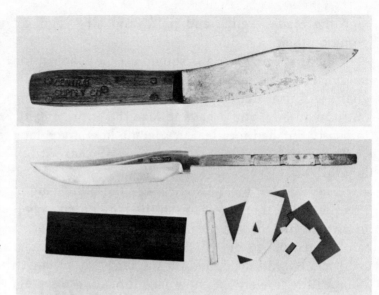

This is the kind of kit Randall used to furnish — a good finished blade, a chunk of wood, a chunk of brass, and some spacers. He doesn't any longer, but some others do.

handles, the basic idea is the same—get it all solidly and squarely together. The result will be oversize and ugly, which is the way it should be.

With all the sharp or near-sharp edges taped, the handle and guard can be hogged down to near-finish by whatever means are at hand. Belt grinders, belt sanders, rasps, and rough-cut files—all or any can be put to work. Once within reach of finish dimension, however, it is best to go slow. At this point, strips of finishing paper are often put to work shoeshine fashion. By varying the width of the strip, nearly all surfaces can be reached. There are not many flat places on the usual handle, but where there are, they can be worked on with the same abrasive, backed by flat pieces of wood.

The professional at this point—and perhaps earlier — would be on his buffing wheel, varying the compounds, to carry the work both to completion and a high degree of brightness. The non-professional is advised to stick with the hand operation, finishing with crocus cloth.

Now, tape the handle and with great care bring the blade surfaces to whatever state of smoothness

All these were assembled by Halter Cunningham in his basement. The top knife, his first, was made with a blade he bought in a gunshop, maker unknown. The next three are Morseth kits. The bottom knife he made with a Randall kit he found. A certain progression of ability is plain to see. Cunningham is pretty good with his hands, although he earns a living with his head.

you require. There is hardly any way to accomplish a bright mirror finish without a buffing wheel and appropriate compounds, and without some danger to the operator. Some fine knife makers do not feel the mirror finish is needed or even desirable.

Making an appropriate sheath for your knife can also be approached in several ways. It is leatherwork, mostly accomplished with the two-needle sewing technique. Finding the materials and tools and instruction is best accomplished by finding a leather-work hobby center. For a single sheath, cutting the available leather to size and shape, gluing it together along the seams, and paying the shoe-repair man to sew it has worked for me. I have also been able to find hobbyists in leather willing to fit a knife into a sheath.

There were two other ways to obtain a non-standard knife mentioned: making a knife from a kit and altering an existing knife.

Most kits provide full instructions of their own. The blades are generally ready for edging as they come, but all the handle work remains. The limitations on the type of knife a fellow can put together this way are few indeed.

I have examined several catalogs and advertisements recently. There must be over a hundred blade shapes and sizes commercially available for making your own knife. Some custom knife makers offer their cataloged designs in kit form, although this changes. Randall has discontinued the practice, for example. In general, though, if you lust for a specific blade with your handle on it, you can probably get it.

How good a blade do you get? Well, most of the commercial offerings are either Solingen or Sheffield. In my judgment, the resulting blades range from averagely good to above average. That means that nearly any of them will make quite useful knives that can be made sufficiently sharp to do work and will retain that sharpness sufficiently well to be practical. They are not extra-fine blades; they do not need to be to do the job.

Sources for blades also offer the trimmings — handle materials of a wide variety, spacers, epoxies, nickel-silver, and brass — as well as hardware like pins, nuts, bolts, and rivets. There are also those establishments that offer the trimmings and hardware but no blades, since they deal with the professional custom-cutlery trade. A fellow with some time and a fairly large city to work in could doubtless find most of what he needs.

In just one catalog, the Golden State Arms booklet, I count thirty-one blade types and styles. Eleven are professional-style butcher's implements ranging from paring knives up to 10-inch steak scimitars. Sixteen are belt knives from 3 to 8 inches, in six or seven general shapes. The others range from a *skean dhu* — a little Scottish stocking knife — to an 11-inch eighteenth-century American rifle knife and a big Arkansas toothpick. There's a carving knife and fork, too. Prices go from $1.25 to $24.50. Most belt patterns go $5 to $10.

And there are fittings. Stag pieces are about $4. Brass guards are about $1. Wood handles are $1 or so. And about $2 buys enough leather for a sheath.

Making a more useful knife out of an existing knife or other tool by modifying the blade is also a possibility. How practical this is would have to be judged on the individual result. However, good steel is available in generally unthought-of forms.

One knife maker of my acquaintance observed to me once that church keys—the beer-can opener before there were pop tops—used to be made of remarkably good steel. This was in the days when a beer can was a redoubtable object made of relatively heavy-gauge steel.

I can generally pick a couple of useful items out of the average home-owner-oriented tool display. Both Sears and Montgomery Ward offer top-of-the-line putty knives I think I could make into good knives— not pretty, but good.

Since there have been swords, they have broken and men have made knives out of the pieces. These tend to be rather more dagger than tool, but definitely knives.

Butcher's implements are the favorite for the remodeler. I have seen a most impressive heavy-duty

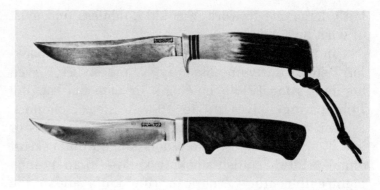

knife made from a large cleaver. Any large knife can be cut down and reshaped, although this does not always lead to happy result since the reshaping may put the new edge and point at a place where the blade is not as hard as it was at the original edge.

From one particular butcher pattern — the one called a sheep skinner—you can get a useful shape by clipping the point on a line almost parallel to the handle. The resulting blade is most useful outdoors.

Clipping the blade — grinding a new line from back to point—alters many knife patterns beneficially. It has to be thought out in advance, but properly done it works. Conversely, some knives are brought to greater utility by shortening the blade and providing a blunter point and more sweep in the edge.

The fellows who fool around making their own knives, and inevitably making more for their friends and family, all say the same thing: Don't expect to do well on the first one. In fact, one recently told me he guessed after he put together three or four dozen he'd get to thinking he was pretty good.

I've seen his knives. He's a surprisingly good craftsman. Why surprising? Well, he's loaded. He drives a Mercedes and is in land syndicates and owns a couple of nice little companies. He used to play a lot of polo and he's gone on safari in Africa several times. He's pretty competent at those things, so perhaps I shouldn't be surprised he can get a handle straight on a purchased blade, but nevertheless I am. You just

This is a Cunningham soldering job at the blade-guard joint. It is pretty good work.

182

don't figure a guy like my friend to go hustling down to his classy suburban basement after dinner to endanger his fingers playing with knives when he could buy any one he wanted, when he could probably buy a knife factory if he took a real notion to do so.

It isn't economy and it isn't the desire for something different that motivates the home knife maker. I think it is the same thing people should buy bench-made knives for—the hand of the maker. It has to be a kick to be using a good tool and know the hand of the maker is your own.

If you make a knife that pleases you outrageously, you could have it etched by Shaw-Leibowitz, whose patterns these are, and who will take on individual work. For the quality of the work, prices are not all that high.

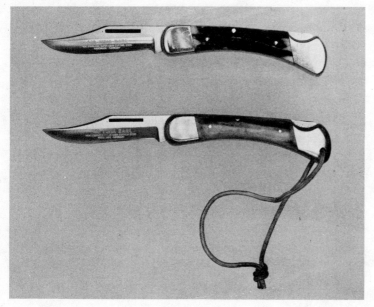

A fellow I knew found this Puma Earl (top) a little angular and boxy to suit him. He thereupon took this expensive knife and ran it down, stag and all, on a belt sander, then buffed it, making it a far more pocketworthy piece. While he was at it, he added a thonghole and is in a position to tell you such holes are best drilled while the surface is still flat.

Epilogue

The King of Norway, the story goes, was once perceived to have a stout knife belted beneath his tailcoat. The occasion was a cultural affair, and some were so bold as to enquire about the knife.

His Majesty remarked, in effect, that a fellow never knows when he might need a good knife.

That was all the excuse the King of Norway needed and that's all the excuse you need.

Index